A Worship Workbook

Related Books on Worship

A Sermon Workbook
by Thomas Troeger and Leonora Tisdale

The Purpose, Pattern, and Character of Worship
by Ed Phillips

Worship Like Jesus
by Constance Cherry

Flow
by Lester Ruth

Liturgies from Below
by Claudio Carvalhaes

Ingenuity
by Lisa Thompson

Gerald C. Liu & Khalia J. Williams

A WORSHIP WORKBOOK

A PRACTICAL GUIDE FOR EXTRAORDINARY LITURGY

Abingdon Press™

Nashville

A WORSHIP WORKBOOK:
A PRACTICAL GUIDE FOR EXTRAORDINARY LITURGY

Copyright © 2021 Abingdon Press

Library of Congress Control Number has been requested.

ISBN: 978-1-5018-9656-9

21 22 23 24 25 26 27 28 29 30—10 9 8 7 6 5 4 3 2 1

MANUFACTURED IN THE UNITED STATES OF AMERICA

CONTENTS

Contents

FOREWORD

Lauren Winner

I picked up *A Worship Workbook* expecting to engage it principally as a scholar who is interested in the history and theology of worship—and while I did occasionally meander down nerdy historical byways (chapter 16's wonderful discussion of Howard Thurman on silence called to mind something I'd recently read about Quakers in eighteenth-century Perquimans County, North Carolina . . .), I found myself reading mostly as a parish priest—that is, as one who is responsible for overseeing and helping God confect worship on Sunday mornings and Wednesday nights for a small band of churchgoers, specifically a small band of small-town, mostly older, mostly white Episcopalians. What is my task, this workbook kept prodding me to ask—what, really, is my task as the leader of that community's worship?

That kind of prodding is one thing this workbook specializes in. It wants to teach you some things, sure—it wants to teach you, for example, that the sacramental rites of English-speaking Anglicans in colonial America helped enshrine this nation's race categories. And it wants to commend specific practices, like attending to the sensory (and not merely the auditory and visual but also the olfactory and tactile) aspects of church worship. It wants to suggest savvy strategies for cycling congregants into new—or *out of* stale—roles in Sunday worship leadership. And it wants to remind you of truths you already know but may have allowed to fade, such as when worshipping, people are always placed in multiple ways—placed in bodies, placed in an ecclesial sanctuary, placed in community, placed on a planet (a planet teeming with life that's also worshipping, all those roaring seas and joyfully shouting forests).

But more fundamentally, this workbook wants to surface insights in and from you. It wants to stimulate ideas, spur actions, and cause you to consider. What surfaced for me, as I read, was that question: as the leader of my community's worship, what's my core task?

Your guides in this reflection, the frighteningly learned and reassuringly wise Khalia Williams and Gerald Liu, suggest that one way to read this book is devotionally, and that's just how I read it—almost as a sort of *lectio divina*. On every page, there's a gem, something unexpected, to catch your imagination (and if you, like me, sometimes find yourself quarreling with this or that bit of richness, so much the better, for neither Christian worship nor the accounts Christians give of it are ever a monotone, a fact reiterated by the very co-authorship of this book, and by Khalia and Gerald's including, as authors of various chapters, several other writers).

Among the riches my mind seized while reading: a Christmas Eve Communion in an English pub; a call for capacious language for and about God coupled with the recognition that "even worn-out words help us worship God in Spirit and in truth"; the recognition that "musical proclamation . . . expresses the desires of God and our desires and actions for God"; the wonderful phrase, new to me, "lyrical attention"; and the astute, tensive recognition that the calendar most readers of this book take for granted "displays the liturgical colonization of time" yet also "shows how our lives count correspondingly to Jesus"—followed by the probing question, "How do we discover unusual theological caution and confidence taking into account the invention of liturgical time and the inseparability of the incarnation no matter how much time passes?" This truly was a *lectio divina* experience for me; the Holy Spirit had something for me in each of those nuggets.

Be warned that this workbook won't only prompt you to think more deeply about worship. A chapter on occasional services included the call for "Services of Blessing for School Teachers and Students." As soon as I read the words, I realized my community will need such a service at the end of the COVID schoolyear during which I was reading and now write. And so, following the spirit of this workbook, I put the book down for a few days and found a few friends to help conject and plot that service. Of course, liturgy-creation in turn provokes more thinking. As my friends and I worked, I became more and more convinced that the church should practice much more of this blessing of local happenings. And not just a blessing of the goodness of our local activities, and not just a return of our accomplishments and efforts to the Lord, though a blessing of teachers and students would be both. Any human activity people are pursuing with anxiety should also receive the community's liturgical blessing, because participation in such a liturgy is exactly a way to bring our anxieties, our concerns, to God.

Planning that service led me back to my possessing question: what is my core task when I am leading worship?

Before reading this book, I might never have asked that question, but if I had, I would have given—or would have thought I should give—an answer principally and explicitly about God, not an answer principally and explicitly about my parishoners. There's plenty in this workbook about God, of course. But there's also a great deal here about people—about people's bodies and people's kinesthetic awareness; about why people squabble with one another; about how people engage the arts; about what disabled people offer and need from their worshipping communities; about what people miss when we enclave with people our own age. As I closed the book after my second time through it, I found myself thinking that worship is anthropological. I found myself thinking about Augustine's insistence that worship doesn't show God anything God doesn't know, and that, because God is always preveniently loving, worship doesn't alter God's attitude toward us. Worship, in this frame, may be construed as being for us, the worshippers. Worship removes obstacles that stand between us and God and, therefore, makes us into the kind of creatures who are more open to God than we would otherwise be. That is, worship makes us more able to receive the love God is already directing toward us. It's worship leaders' great privilege to assist people in thus becoming more receptive of God's love.

Much of the time, worshippers (and even worship leaders) are either grieving, distracted, or bored; the ideal of attentive piety is rarely instanced. How should people in that condition—grieving, distracted, bored—be addressed as worshippers? Maybe next year, or in five years, I'll differently understand and differently articulate my core task, but at this moment, the clarity Khalia and Gerald summoned from me is that my task as a worship leader is simply to help worshippers find a way in to worship from wherever they've been; and then stay with them while they're in this activity of worship, this landscape of praise, confession, petition, and lament; and then help them find a way out, back to the world, ideally more attentive to truth and more receptive of love than they were when they arrived. I'm grateful for the ways this book will help me do that, and I'm curious about what it will help you do as you continue in your call to lead others to worship the Lord in the beauty of holiness.

ACKNOWLEDGMENTS

Co-authored books are sometimes born out of relationships that have marinated for a long time. Khalia and I had just met when we decided to embark on this project together. Our collaboration is as fresh as the ideas we present in the pages that follow. We offer new wine to quench congregations and communities of faith thirsting for more expansive, more welcoming, and more woke worship leadership and liturgical practice. We thank you, the reader, first for trying something new. And we hope that what we have wrought will embolden, empower, and enliven the work of the people under your liturgical care.

We would also like to thank the many students of worship that we have taught. This expansive network of students spans across the country and over several years of engagement. Every group of students brings with them new energy, questions, and discovery. They have inspired us, challenged us, and brought new ideas and hope to our worship work and teaching.

In addition, we give God thanks for the communities who have shaped, supported, and given us room to develop our vision for worship. For those at Trevecca Nazarene University, Andover Newton Theological Seminary (when we still met at the hilltop campus in Newton Center), Louisville Presbyterian Theological School, Drew Theological School, Princeton Theological Seminary, American Baptist Seminary of the West, Pacific School of Religion, Columbia Theological Seminary, and Candler School of Theology. We are also eternally grateful for the pastors and congregations across the Greater New Jersey, Mississippi, and Tennessee United Methodist Annual Conferences; the Christian Church (Disciples of Christ); Providence Missionary Baptist Church; and the many churches throughout South Florida who have been partners in worship and entrusted our leadership and innovation. Dreams for your ministries are the primary inspiration for our search and articulation of what makes worship extraordinary.

We also extend our thanks for research assistants and teaching assistants in worship, and student worship coordinators. Gerald thanks Chris Jorgensen, Sharon Hausman, Sam Gilmore, Leanne Ketcham, Victor Koon, Emily Lueder, and Holly Bailey. Khalia thanks Byron Wratee, Stephanie Milton, and Jacob Cogman, who have been invaluable thought partners along the journey. How would we have managed without all of your help?

Christy Bonner, thank you for pouring through every page before we sent it off to the publisher. Connie Stella, thank you for believing in the project and helping us stay the course even as a pandemic struck. Katie Johnston, your editing hand made the *Workbook* shine. Thank you.

Finally, we want to thank all of the contributors to this work. To Leah Schade, Rebecca Spurrier, Stephanie Budwey, Lis Valle-Ruiz, Andrew Wymer, Safwat Marzouk, Emily Lueder, and Chris Jorgensen. We are indebted to each of you for your wisdom, especially as you poured into our work from your own ministry in the midst of a pandemic. Your partnership and collaboration is a gift to this work and to the future of worship. We are indebted to you each.

Finally, we thank our family and friends who have been with us during the tireless hours of writing, brainstorming, conference calls, and so much more that it took to complete *A Worship Workbook*. I, Khalia, especially thank my husband, Damon Williams, for being my greatest encourager and motivator. Your unending support has enriched my life beyond measure. I, Gerald, want to dedicate my part in this collaboration to Cleo LaRue, Princeton Theological Seminary Preaching Professor Extraordinaire, colleague of colleagues, confidant and dear friend, who stood by me and relentlessly cut a path forward when I know he had far better and more important things to do.

Khalia Williams, there would be no *Worship Workbook* without you. I, Gerald, am grateful for your friendship at every step as well as your liturgical finesse and fortitude.

Gerald Liu, I cannot express the joy it has been to walk with you through this project. I am thankful to God that our paths crossed, and that we were able to birth not only a new work, but an amazing new friendship along the way. Thank you for the gift that you are to the academy and the church.

THE WORK OF THE PEOPLE

Welcome to *A Worship Workbook*, conceived as a companion to *A Sermon Workbook: Exercises in the Art and Craft of Preaching* (Abingdon, 2013) by Thomas H. Troeger and Leonora Tubbs Tisdale. *A Sermon Workbook* was "designed to help you think like a preacher, write like a preacher, and proclaim the good news with imagination, theological integrity, deepened biblical insight, and heartfelt passion."[1] It harvested knowledge from years of Introduction to Preaching classes at Yale Divinity School. Like *A Sermon Workbook*, *A Worship Workbook* aims to help you think, write, and act like a worship leader. We also want to resource an array of Christian worship leaders—from new pastors to seasoned clergy serving one or multiple congregations, directors of worship and music leaders, lay leaders/those on a worship design team, as well as students in theological education and church members. The questions and exercises you will encounter in this workbook are designed to help you think deeply about worship leadership and its theological impact within your particular ministry context, and enliven worship planning and leadership in a hands-on way.

Over the years, as we have worked with congregations, we have noticed a need for more robust worship leadership. We have encountered pastoral leaders who feel unprepared, unequipped, and even fearful to provide such leadership. The collaboration of *A Worship Workbook* seeks to embolden leaders to be ready, resourceful, and brave in their liturgical leadership, by centering the particularity of context, human difference, and the revelation of God as valuable starting points for planning, leading, and assessing worship. The pages that follow aim to stretch your liturgical imagination and practice so that you can lead worship with exceptional theological acumen and cultural dexterity.

Who We Are

This workbook has been written as an ecumenical, cross-institutional collaboration between two colleagues who themselves embody human difference in worship leadership. Khalia is the first African American woman to serve as the assistant dean of worship and music at Emory University's Candler School of Theology, and Gerald was the first American-born and tenure-track Asian American professor of worship and preaching at Princeton Theological Seminary. Before becoming theological educators, we have led worship as youth, associate, and lead pastor, liturgical artist and musician, and guest consultant within a plethora of contexts for laity and clergy from a variety of generations from the newly born to the dearly departed.

Public worship leadership remains a key component in our current academic posts. Deep engagement in worship for academic institutions and church congregations has given us insight into multiple liturgical practices and raised many questions and ideas for envisioning and enacting faithful and exceptional worship into the future. While *A Worship Workbook* represents some of what we think are best practices for worship leaders across diverse contexts, we acknowledge that we too are continually refining and tinkering, in conversation with others, what fruitful Christian worship can be. Please feel free, therefore, to reach out to us by searching for our contact information online if you have ideas about strengthening the leadership of worship.

The Structure of the Workbook

The content of the workbook is divided into two main parts: (1) Widening Our Worship Imagination, and (2) Deepening the Work of the People. We encourage you to use both sections to pry open broader thinking about your own ministry contexts and more expansive imagination for new ways of being in worship.

Part 1 focuses on broadening conceptions of history and time, scripture, sacred texts, inter-religious dialogue, the sacraments, preaching, weddings, funerals, other occasional services, and sacred space. We rethink worship habits (such as the puzzling preference to rely upon two patterns of worship) and reconsider liturgical language (what it is that we say and how we say it). Part 2 begins with exploring dynamics of embodiment. It also introduces guest contributors who regale us with knowledge about worship and the need for it to engage disability, gender and sexuality, Latinx liturgical sensibilities, the normativity of whiteness, and intercultural awareness. You'll also find contributions from a chaplain and a pastor who wrestle with the new reality that worship must sometimes occur in disembodied ways as a result of unpredictable scenarios (like a pandemic) and give us hopeful advice into the unfolding future liturgy as a shared endeavor. In addition, Part 2 explores liturgical horizons such as the need for more intergenerational worship. We examine the magic of liturgical wonder, the joy of congregational gifts, the concern of congregational resistance, and the beauty of worship artistry and musicality—not only during a service as it happens but also in the planning of worship collaboratively and individually. We conclude with a constellation of questions related to relevance as a challenge that any skilled leader of worship dare not ignore, and we suggest that dependence upon the revelation of God helps us craft worship able to address and touch any day and age.

How to Use This Workbook

Commendable introductory textbooks in worship already exist for new leaders. This workbook is primarily written for practitioners already actively leading worship, both lay and ordained. It aims to help a worship team or a solo leader excel in deeper reflection and planning in order to mine more out of existing patterns of worship and to invent new ones as needed. *A Worship Workbook* is designed for immediate application, in live liturgical settings as well as classroom spaces.

1. Worship Design as a Worship Team

If you are using this book with a worship planning team, we suggest reading it one chapter at a time. There is a lot of information to process. The workbook will incite even greater creativity and discussion among your team if it is approached gradually. Since each chapter stands alone, you can begin with the chapters according to your needs and expand from there. Perhaps begin with the areas that pose major obstacles or those that show great promise and opportunity. Use the questions and exercises to guide your conversation or as a conversation starter to your planning meetings as you prayerfully walk through each chapter.

2. Reflection and Devotion for Worship Leadership

A Worship Workbook can also be engaged devotionally. The questions and exercises might lead to journaling particular thoughts, feelings, and ideas that shed light upon past worship experiences as well as hopes for future growth and transformation. In reading *A Worship Workbook* devotionally, we still recommend finding conversation partners. You may want to create a discussion group. Perhaps offer discussion of the *Workbook* as an offering of Christian education in your community of faith.

3. Conversations in an Introductory Worship Course

Theological education is not strictly a classroom exercise. Many students journey through the academic experience as practitioners. A number of programs require students to be deeply involved in congregational life and work as a curriculum requirement. This workbook invites deeper conversation to connect what is learned in the classroom to what students are living out in parishes by providing alongside each chapter questions and exercises to generate new and creative ideas for class discussions and public liturgical engagement.

Overall, we want to invigorate the leadership of Christian worship right now. Some of the questions are intended to produce responses that lead to immediate practice. Others call for more reflection and operate in a devotional manner. In either case, the questions and exercises here concern themselves less with coverage and more with questions and exercises of worship leadership that can be applied swiftly, and that we believe are urgently needed to display the love, justice, mercy, and hope that God desires we continually share with one another.

What We Mean by Liturgy

Liturgy is typically associated with "high" or prayer book forms of worship. Yet what we mean by liturgy has a longer history than any Christian tradition and encompasses practices uncontainable by any particular Christian church. From here onward, liturgy means what is worked out and wrought by ordinary but called folks like you and us. The political theorist and liturgy aficionado Giorgio Agamben reminds us that the word *liturgy* had a civic meaning long before it had a theological one. It originally described service for the people in Greco-Roman culture.[2] Liturgy encompassed public theater, public games, parades, and even mundane activities like making sure trash was picked up. Back then, the wealthy were tasked with performing *leitourgia*, which translated from Greek into English means "work of the people." Not until the translation of the Old Testament into Greek in the third century BCE does *leitourgia*, or liturgy, take on sacred meaning. It was a substitute for the Hebrew word *sheret*, which means "to serve" or "to help." The originary civic meaning of liturgy courses underneath the understanding of liturgy in this book. Except that in the following pages, liturgy is not an activity undertaken by the privileged. We invite all who feel called to lead liturgy, and to continue the tradition of positioning liturgy as service to the public in a variety of forms. Liturgy is therefore broadly defined here, and is more or less interchangeable and synonymous with the word *worship*. Liturgy and worship are the primary activities of congregations. They happen within congregations, and beyond them as well. And they are always evolving.

Why This Workbook?

This text is designed to spark liturgical imagination. As Norwegian novelist Karl Ove Knausgaard writes in *My Struggle*, "Not all rituals involve ceremonies, not all rituals are rigidly demarcated, there are those that take shape in the midst of everyday life and are recognizable by the weight and charge they give the otherwise normal event."[3] We want to help you dream and invent for liturgy as well as think and act upon it. This text is designed to help worship leaders champion justice. Emilie Townes has said that it is impossible to call on hope without first naming what is evil. Naming what is evil may seem like a depressing activity to do during worship, but evil is already at hand in the foundations of Christian worship. The baptism of Jesus begins with a refusal from John and concludes with a famished journey of satanic temptation in the wilderness. At the table of the Last Supper, the betrayal of Judas crackles through indirect dinner conversation, exposing what Karl Barth calls negative discipleship, the eventual selling of Jesus into the hands of oppressors instead of delivering sinners into the patient mercy of the Messiah.[4] We hope that the thinking undertaken in the pages that follow will expand into further transformative theories and acts of worship that question what the goods of current worship practices are, as well as compel leaders of worship to keep tinkering with worship as we know it so that it shines ever more brightly with love for all parishioners and neighbors. This book hopes to be your helpful guide.

Part One

WIDENING OUR WORSHIP
IMAGINATION

WHAT MAKES FOR GOOD WORSHIP?

If you are reading this workbook, you probably have a sense for what good worship is. Maybe it is mostly a sense, because you have not put words toward it. Perhaps this is because you have grown up going to church, and the transition to planning and implementing good worship intentionally as a worship leader is trickier than you thought. Maybe you have not yet experienced good worship exactly as you intuit or imagine. Maybe you have worshipped like a liturgical nomad so far, searching for the right ritual fit and landing in some congregations that came close or that may have been just what you were looking for, only to find yourself back on the search for various reasons—moving for school, a job, a partner, a scandal, a disagreement, a wound, or just because. Maybe you have participated in good worship. Yet you are not quite sure how to set conditions for it on a consistent basis. Maybe Christianity is new to you. Or maybe you have been running from a call that has finally caught up with you. Maybe you have been so inspired or so underwhelmed that you know you can offer good worship, and that you can do better. Maybe you are a seasoned leader of worship interested in expanding your expertise. Either way, this book is one of many arrows that you'll collect in your quiver so you can aim for liturgical excellence.

We enter this chapter assuming that you have already been thinking about preaching, and have established a sense for what good worship looks, feels, and sounds like. We want to begin with a chapter that helps worship leaders ponder over what makes for effective worship, and crystallize what weakens worship so that you can avoid those pitfalls. The questions and exercises in this chapter are intended to help you identify what makes worship sing, so you know what "notes" generate the most theological impact. In other words, what are the key elements in worship that make for the most impressive theological engagement? Is it close alignment with a biblical text or theme? Is it professionalism in the choir or poise among the readers and liturgists? Is it decorum or simplicity? Is it freedom or form? Is it a range of characteristics and more? By complement, when worship leaders zero in on what makes worship wither as well and put that into words, they can pay better attention to what convolutes or undermines creating conditions for holy encounter. Do we need to check our denominational or personal hubris regarding what is liturgically correct? Do we need to ensure that those leading worship are not either culturally or generationally homogenous, or both? Do we need to ask if good worship is limited only to what can happen within a sanctuary? Or are there possibilities in the public sphere and the World Wide Web? When we name what we think makes for meaningful and underwhelming worship, then we have starting points for sketching clearer designs of worship that glorify God and celebrate the love of God and neighbor.

Importantly, the chapter here puts the onus on criteria generated by you. We would be remiss to offer *A Worship Workbook* without creating space within it for what *you* think and know about emboldening Christian worship. Whether you are a veteran of leading worship or a newbie, this chapter will help each kind of reader draw out into words a trove of liturgical wisdom.

Questions and Exercises

1. Think of one of the most meaningful experiences of worship that you have had. It may have been a special service or an ordinary one in your local church; an occasion of worship as a visitor in a congregation; a time of worship during a retreat, concert, conference; or another kind of event. It may have occurred in solitude, in nature, or during a moment of awe or personal illumination not at all affiliated with Christianity in any way. In a few sentences, reflect upon why that experience of worship was so meaningful to you. What made it that way? Try to recall and consider different dimensions including but not limited to the order of worship, prayers, rituals, space, bodily kinesthetics, smells, bells, and use of the arts. Try to be as detailed as possible.

2. Think of the most underwhelming experiences of worship that you have had. In a sentence or two, reflect upon why that experience of worship was so disappointing. What made it that way? Was it poorly executed? Was it exclusive or socially insensitive? Try to recall and consider different dimensions including but not limited to the order of worship, prayers, rituals, space, bodily kinesthetics, smells, bells, and use of the arts. Try to be as detailed as possible.

3. Complete the following sentences:

    I believe worship is most efficacious when . . .

    I believe worship is most negligent when . . .

    I believe worship is "lukewarm" or "so-so" when . . .

Individual and Small Group Reflection and Discussion

After you have answered the above questions individually, share them with colleagues in person, over the phone, or online, and ask them how they might answer. If you are using the workbook in a class setting, gather into groups in real time or in a group thread or video chat, and share your answers with one another.

After sharing answers to the first set of questions, you may want to distill your discussion into a list of key facets of meaningful worship.

1. What are the main ingredients of meaningful worship? Try to be as concise as possible here.

2. Based upon the list created from question 1 and your answers above, what kind of rubric could you create, what kind of criteria could you name, to check to see if your worship leading has the hallmarks of good worship?

Follow Up: What Students Have to Say

At the start of each year, I (Khalia) assemble a team of sixteen students to lead the worship life at Candler School of Theology for the academic year. These students are an intentionally diverse group that brings together graduate students from different denominational affiliations, racial/ethnic backgrounds, geographic regions, ages, and theological sensitivities. In our first meeting, which is generally focused on orientation and training, these students are asked, "What is good worship for you?" I use this question as a way to help students hear the diverse responses in the room, and it is an eye-opening experience for many. In addition, I use this same question when leading workshops within congregations and pastoral leaders on embodied worship. Serving as an icebreaker, the participants are broken into small groups to think through their understanding of "good worship" and are then asked to describe what they heard, and where there were similarities and differences. Below is an abbreviated list developed from the last three years of engaging this exercise with the Candler School of Theology worship students, and the church workshops.

Students' Responses to the Question, What Is Good Worship for You?

1. Music
Music that is centering and reflective.
Energetic and exciting sound.

Invites the community to sing together. There is nothing more beautiful than hearing the people around you singing in harmony with you.

Traditional music—hymns that have a history, that make me think about my grandmother.

Songs that soothe the soul.

Good contemporary music and anthems that make me want to sing.

Moments of silence.

Theologically accurate music.

Intentional music.

Blend of sound that includes favorite songs of the church and new songs to learn.

Variety of genres to connect with everyone who is gathered.

2. Congregational Engagement

Worship that leads the congregation into a deeper connection with God.

Worship that is shaped around community.

Invites participation of people in the pews.

Moves through different ways of being active in the experience—I can move, I can be silent, I can sing, I can pray.

Worship that is put together with the members in mind. It is apparent when the worship leaders know their audience and connect with them.

A celebration! We come together to celebrate God.

Offers opportunities for the people to be heard—testimony, scripture reading, or any way that lets more than the pastor be heard.

Times for lament as a church family—litanies, prayers, silence. Being able to lament in a community has been transformative.

Communal rituals beyond Communion and baptism.

Connection to the doctrine and foundation of the church through different practices (prayers, Communion liturgies, and seasonal celebrations).

3. Incites Action beyond the Moment

Makes me think about the way I exist in the world.

Gives me something to carry with me through the week; things to think about in living out my faith.

Engages relevant issues and makes the congregation aware of injustices in the world and our role to fight against them.

Not just a "feel-good" moment, but a time when the church comes together and is motivated to be God's hands and feet in the world.

Inspires me to be better and do better, because that is what God requires of me.

Worshipping outside of the sanctuary in the community.

Justice-centered worship; not afraid to address social issues in a worshipful way.

4. Worship Environment

The place where I want to go to be with God and with others. It is different from my personal devotion.

Welcoming and hospitable from the parking lot to the sanctuary.

Visually appealing space—connects with the season of the church, even in the small ways, and is a nice environment.

Mindfulness of all who are in the building, and those who are online. Making this clear throughout the service.

Invitational environment.

Two separate services that offer two different styles of worship—traditional and contemporary.

Good use of technology.

Opportunities for fellowship.

A space created for the community.

5. Dynamic Worship Leaders

Having people lead worship who can read the room and know where to take the service, and who are in tune with how the Holy Spirit is moving and can flow.

A good preacher is key for good worship. That is the main part of the service that many people show up for, so the preaching has to be good.

Leaders who liturgically heighten the service through their presence and presentation.

Pleasant people in the pulpit—smiles, warm personality, connectable.

Creative and diverse leaders.

Seamlessly weaves together what is important to the community with what God is doing in the moment.

THE MYSTERY OF OUR JEWISH ROOTS

Christian worship is rooted in Judaism. John Gager writes that "in virtually every corner of early Christian culture, Jewish influence makes its presence known: liturgy, holidays, theology, Christology, eschatology, communal life and leadership, ethics, the Bible and biblical interpretation, art, and more."[1] Christian worship would not exist without Judaism. And it continues to pulse with liturgical know-how inherited from Judaism. Therefore, skilled leadership of Christian worship must engage Judaism or risk self-absorption, tautology, and even prejudice and violence in the form of supersessionism and anti-Semitism. Yet identifying exactly where the connections are and how they developed confounds scholars of liturgy to this day.

Christian worship hardly resembles its Jewish past. Family likenesses with contemporary Jewish worship are also faint at best. Yet Jesus was a Jew. The disciples were Jews. Paul was a Jew. The first believers were Jews. Jewish women ran the households where Christian worship first took place.[2] The first scriptures came from the Septuagint (second century BCE), a Greek translation of Jewish or Hebrew scriptures. In fact, the entire canon of scripture consists of writings identified with Jewish authorship.[3] The eldest New Testament text, 1 Thessalonians (50 CE), is a letter from a Jewish author, the Apostle Paul. The latest New Testament writing is not the book of Revelation, but 2 Peter (125 CE?), which is likely written pseudonymously, with authorship associated with or written in the name of Peter, a Jewish author. We lose touch with who we are when we neglect our Jewish origins in Christian worship today.

Exploring and celebrating Jewish heritage in the context of Christian worship amounts to more than a liturgical walk down memory lane. Jews have been relentlessly persecuted throughout the evolution of Christian worship. Consider the Slaughter of the Innocents in Matthew 2:16. The violence recounted there clearly targets the Jews whether or not the massacre actually occurred. When Paul addresses who is "weak" and "strong" in Romans 14, he is in part dealing with Gentiles torn about how to welcome returning Jewish leaders and Jewish adherents of Christian house churches who were previously expelled from Rome by Emperor Claudius (49 CE). The fourth-century preacher John Chrysostom, *chryso-stom* literally meaning "golden-mouthed," likened the synagogue to a "brothel," "a den of robbers and a lodging of wild beasts," and demonic: "But when God forsakes a people, what hope of salvation is left? When God forsakes a place, that place becomes the dwelling of demons."[4] In *The Darkening Age: The Christian Destruction of the Classical*

World, Catherine Nixey tells us that Nazi Germany relished reprinting Chrysostom's sermons.[5] Even the best of Christian preaching has not only forgotten our Jewish heritage, but blasphemed it as well.

In *The Dangers of Christian Practice: On Wayward Gifts, Characteristic Damage, and Sin*, Lauren Winner retells how a rumor that Jews threw a pebble at a monstrance, a transparent display of the eucharistic host, led to the slaughter of Jews in Prague in 1389.[6] When Christian preaching and worship forget how vital the mystery of our Jewish roots are to who we are in God and how Judaism is at the root of how we glorify God and love one another in prayer, sacrament, ritual, song, sermon, media, and more, we risk wiping away not only history, but the people of God. There are several Christian traditions who officially stand against anti-Judaism including the Roman Catholic Church, the Presbyterian Church (USA), the United Church of Christ, and The United Methodist Church. Yet church-going individuals have ravaged synagogues with shootings.[7] Anti-Semitism and supersessionism, or "the belief that the New Testament covenant supersedes the Mosaic covenant of the Hebrew Bible, and that the Christian Church has displaced Israel as God's chosen people," are not the only risks.[8] Anachronism is also a risk. We end up reading Jesus, the disciples, Paul, and a host of other Jewish figures in the Bible as if they were Christians. The gospel does not negate Judaism. It thrives in relationship with it.

Remember, for example, that Matthew begins by locating Jesus the Messiah as the son of David, the son of Abraham (Matthew 1), and at the cross Jesus is declared King of the Jews (Matthew 27:37). By resourcing and investigating the rich Jewish history of Christianity, we realize that our faith comes from another nation and people. We begin to see how far we have developed from that history, and how far we will continue to evolve through Jewish and Christian dialogue and interreligious and intercultural dialogue of all kinds in ways that marvel our imaginations and define new futures of Christian worship that we could hardly predict or conceive.

Questions and Exercises

1. How does our view of God change when we recognize how much of Christianity is rooted in Judaism? For example, the Gospel of Matthew links Jesus to the lineage of David. Jesus also focuses exclusively upon "the lost sheep of the house of Israel" until the last paragraph of chapter 28, which most scholars believe is an addition to the text. How does taking seriously the Jewishness of Jesus compel us to find ways for more learning and dialogue with Jewish neighbors in Christian worship and prevent us from worshipping as if what happens in Christian worship replaces Judaism?

2. In antiquity, synagogues were where non-Jews, Christians, and pagans gathered. At least half of the attendants in some synagogues were non-Jews. How might Christian churches, as heirs of Judaism, also create space within worship for interreligious and intercultural dialogue?

3. Visit a synagogue service individually or as a congregation. Befriend the people there. Invite a rabbi to church and even to share a message with the congregation during worship. When Passover appears in biblical readings or during the season of Hanukkah, which often overlaps with Advent, many Christian congregations celebrate Sukkot or Shabbat dinners. What would it look like to celebrate some Jewish holidays with Jewish neighbors?

4. Only 20 percent of the Old Testament appears in the lectionary, a calendar of assigned biblical readings for churches worldwide. One starting point within already existing sources of Christian worship for deeper engagement with Judaism is to converse with the entirety of the Old Testament in Christian worship. In addition to preaching, reading, singing, ritualizing, and praying from Old Testament texts, how might our sense of mystery and history expand in Christian worship if we read or learned to read the Old Testament in Hebrew?

5. If a Hebrew speaker is unavailable within the church, establish a friendship with a Hebrew-speaking neighbor, perhaps from a nearby synagogue or seminary. Or if an educator is available to assist the church, make the learning of Hebrew a part of the church's Christian education. Resources online such as the Jewish Virtual Library (jewishvirtual library.org) and the Blue Letter Bible (blueletterbible.org) also provide good points of entry regarding Jewish history, culture, and politics in relationship to the United States, as well as biblical Hebrew translation and pronunciation resources.

LITURGICAL TIME

Christian churches are known for two holidays: Christmas and Easter. Their dates, however, vary by denominations. Many Orthodox communities follow the Julian calendar (46 BC), an older timetable that lags thirteen days behind the younger but more widely observed Gregorian calendar (1582 CE). The difference between the two results from Pope Gregory XIII attempting to recalibrate the Julian calendar as it drifted from reliably corresponding to seasons and equinoxes. Christmas thus falls on December 25 according to the Gregorian calendar and January 7 according to the Julian calendar. Easter celebrations coincide between the two calendars only on occasional years, but can differ from as much as one to five weeks between the two modes of tracking time. Even still, celebrating the resurrection never stretches beyond days between April 4 and May 8 for the Orthodox.

The asynchrony between churches following the Gregorian and Julian calendars complicates any discussion of liturgical time. Yet zooming out from the calendrical idiosyncrasies in determining particular dates associated with the birth and resurrection of Jesus, we can see without too much calculation how in each year, liturgical time frames the nativity and new life of Christ:

ADVENT
FOUR SUNDAYS BEFORE CHRISTMAS

The season encourages preparation for the coming of Christ. Adventus means "coming."

CHRISTMAS

EPIPHANY
JANUARY 6 IS A CUSTOMARY DATE.

From the fourth century, Epiphany has celebrated the baptism of Jesus, the nativity, the visit of the magi, and the wedding feast in Cana where Jesus turned water into wine.

LENT
APPROXIMATELY FORTY DAYS

Ash Wednesday:
The beginning of Lent and often a day of fasting. Congregants are asked to remember their human mortality in the face of God's eternal love. Traditionally, ashes are imposed in the shape of a cross upon the foreheads of the faithful. The cleric may accompany the gesture by declaring, "From dust you came, to dust you shall return" or "Repent, and believe the good news."

Holy Week or Great Week:
The closing week of Lent.

Palm Sunday:
The first Sunday of Holy Week. Churches often include the waving of palms in worship to commemorate Jesus entering Jerusalem on a donkey and crowds waving palm branches with shouts of "Hosanna!"

Maundy Thursday:
Maundy comes from a medieval English rendering of the Latin word *mandatum*, which means "command." The observance of Holy or Maundy Thursday, however, dates back much earlier than medieval times, at least to the fourth century. On this day, the feet of clerics and paupers were washed by a presiding bishop, abbot, or priest. Alms, which came to be known as Maundy money, were also often given. Today, churches often include rituals of footwashing, the Eucharist, stripping of the altar and other liturgical furnishings, and evening services such as tenebrae, which ends with the gradual extinguishing of candles.

Good Friday:
Christians remember the crucifixion on this day through various liturgical services and rites, and fasting. Often, a passion narrative is read, the cross is venerated, and Communion is served. Anti-Semitic overtones have appeared in historical celebrations of Good Friday as the Jews were blamed for the death of Jesus. After Vatican II, these instances of blame were excised. Some congregations offer Stations of the Cross, fourteen representations of Jesus's journey to the cross, for meditation and prayer.

Holy Saturday:
The day before Easter and often a day of fasting. Some congregations host evening vigils to prepare for Easter morning, which may include baptism, confirmation, and a concluding Eucharist.

EASTER

ASCENSION DAY
FORTIETH DAY AFTER EASTER (THURSDAY) OR SUNDAY BEFORE PENTECOST

Ascension day celebrations date back to the fourth century. Churches remember the risen Christ ascending to heaven as found in Luke 24:50-52 and Acts 1:9-10.

PENTECOST
SEVENTH SUNDAY AFTER EASTER

Pentecost closes a fifty-day span and marks the fiftieth day of the Easter season. It dates back to the second century and its name comes from a Greek word meaning "fiftieth." In England today, churches there call Pentecost Whitsunday. Christians everywhere celebrate Pentecost by giving thanks for the gift of the Holy Spirit as found in Acts 2:2-4. Pentecost has Jewish roots in the Feast of Weeks, following Passover (Tobit 2:1 and 2 Maccabees 12:32).[1]

ORDINARY TIME

Ordinary time denotes periods in the liturgical year that lie outside the principal seasons. The primary designations for ordinary time span from the end of Christmas or Epiphany to the beginning of Lent and from Pentecost to Advent.

Liturgical time encompasses far more than the high points of Christmas and Easter and major stretches of liturgical time that knit them together. Feasts and Holy days exceed what is listed here. Worship also blooms beyond weekly gatherings, whether they fall on a Sunday or some other day during the week. Worship unfolds all across time. In fact, liturgical time, or marking time according to worship associated with and observed by Jesus, goes back millennia, long before Julian and Gregorian calendars. It has Jewish roots in Israelite history that precede the birth of Christ by at least another thirteen hundred years.[1] The Gospel of John makes the point more emphatically, placing Jesus chronologically as the Word with God and that was God *in the beginning*. Liturgical time, as observance of time to glorify God, in a way, starts with the very recognition of time itself. Liturgical time, as sacred time wrought by the people of God, is human-made, formalized by dates and calendars that demarcate it in various Christian traditions. Yet simultaneously, it is, paradoxically, of the divine.

Therefore, liturgical innovation and creativity can include new ways of ordering time. Christian feasts and high holy days have specific dates. Yet we can also choose to celebrate Christian feasts, high holy days, and more on any day at any time. Choosing new ways to sacralize time in the name of Christ does not dismiss the significance of liturgical time as we know it. Rather, it is an expression of evolving faithfulness in God and to the churches of God.

Consider the time we now call the Common Era. A monk named Dionysius Exiguus (Denys the Little, AD 470–544), born in Scythia, what is now Dobruja, a territory shared by Romania and Bulgaria, and who worked in Rome from approximately 500–540, developed what we know as the Common Era, or what was historically called *Anno Domini Nostri Jesu Christi* ("In the year of our Lord Jesus Christ"), as a date for the incarnation, to unify celebrations for Easter. His calculations remain unverifiable. They derive from sources and reasoning about which we can only speculate. Dionysius Exiguus never intended for his computation to have more than a liturgical function. Yet his innovation provided not only a common starting point of reference for the Julian and Gregorian calendars, it organized our years with uniformity around the world according to the birth of the Messiah.[2] Ever since Isaac Newton used the correlative BC to number the years in his *Chronology of Ancient Kingdoms Amended* (1728), AD and BC or CE and BCE have become standard ways of marking time. On the one hand, what we now call the Common Era displays the liturgical colonization of time. On the other hand, it shows how our lives count correspondingly to Jesus in any given year. How do we discover unusual theological caution and confidence taking into account the invention of liturgical time and the inseparability of the incarnation no matter how much time passes?

Questions and Exercises

1. In addition to scheduling or stylizing worship according to a particular liturgical season or feast, like Advent and Christmas or Lent and Easter, how might you continue the tradition of inventing new ways to count time as sacred and liturgical?

2. In worship, how is it possible to craft a particular experience of time, in terms of pace or tempo, paying attention to the rhythm of our lives within and outside any given occasion of worship? How can the rate of speech, the inclusion of silence, the rhythm and

pitch of music, the brightness and contrast of light, the colors of liturgical paraments, and arrangements of liturgical furnishings and adornment create different experiences of holy time? What other materials or experiences of worship can be adjusted in order to create fresh or more intentional experiences of time as sacred and liturgical?

3. If liturgical time ultimately serves the purposes of God, what would it look like to structure and plan worship toward the *eschaton*, and not only the incarnation as celebrated on Christmas Day and the resurrection as celebrated on Easter Day? Jesus was born, raised, gave us the Holy Spirit, and ascended long ago. Chronologically, we as churches and communities of faith worship in the time after Christmas, Easter, Pentecost, and Ascension Day. What would it look like to organize liturgical time as a church chronology counting down to the future of God? Does a new liturgical translucence result when we inform familiar cycles of sacred time with the still-unfolding future of God?

Chapter 4

TRADITION

When we think of the word *tradition* in terms of Christian worship, what do we mean? Do denominational identity and method come to mind? Does the word *tradition* evoke ecclesial authority or the communion of saints? Do we imagine Roman basilicas and Greek cathedrals? Or does it conjure more intimate gatherings where a home becomes a sanctuary for sacred celebrations of ritual proclamation, bath, meal, and prayer? Is tradition a gold mine of liturgical wisdom? Or is it a quarry of fossils and old bones or that transmission of sacred skeletons from one time and place to another?

However we think of tradition, it is important to realize that Christian worship has been multi-linear, and multicultural and intercultural from its inception. What we call Christian worship has roots in Jewish rites and Sabbath meals. It defined itself amid a polytheistic culture described in the New Testament and from there took on new shapes in a wide variety of homes in Jerusalem, Palestine, Syria (including what is now Iraq, Iran, and Turkey), Egypt, North Africa, and more, before filling public halls across the Greco-Roman world. Worship became Latinized and Orthodox. Many centuries later, Reformers reinvented the tradition of Christian worship. Colonialists, slaves, the converted, and ordinary citizens made it their own as new lands were discovered. Modern liturgical and ecumenical movements have sought to refine and distill what tradition essentially means. Cultural, biblical, and patristic scholarship over thousands of years and across an array of languages and lands has also clarified what worship traditions have actually been and what we have imagined them to be. This kind of growth reflects what Maxwell E. Johnson has already written, that tradition is not *Heilgeschichte*, a monolinear unbroken liturgical history.[1] Tradition is "in motion," to borrow a phrase from Robert Taft.[2]

Even early sources of Christian liturgy such as the Apostolic Tradition tell us so little about the first three centuries of Christian worship. Johnson states elsewhere that the Didache, which describes the earliest rites of Christian initiation beyond the New Testament itself, provides information "only of the most general kind."[3] For example, while the Apostolic Tradition provides directions regarding the appropriate order and etiquette for baptizands depending upon their age (children should be baptized first, their parents should speak on their behalf if they are unable to speak; then the "old men"; then the women without any "ornaments" and with hair loosened), and that they should enter the water alone, we do not know to what extent communities followed those specific instructions. Furthermore, scholars question whether the Apostolic Tradition is a third-century document. They believe that the baptismal instructions it contains are a composite sketch that may not reflect actual Roman practices.[4]

The Didache describes a meal practice. Yet it does not associate its elements with the body and blood of Christ. Scholars question whether the Didache actually describes a Eucharist even though the word *eucharistia* or "thanksgiving" is used in its depiction.[5] It appears that meal celebrations resembling what we know as the Eucharist now varied widely in the early centuries of Christian worship. The fogginess of the past, however, does not lead to liturgical relativism. Rather, coming to terms with the fact that traditions of Christian worship have evolved over time from many vectors of cultural and ecclesial influence around the world gives Christian worship leaders today freedom to continue liturgical experimentation and innovation as practices of faith and in practices of faith in order to discover more effective ways for bearing witness to the love and mercy of God.

Indeed, Christian leaders have already reconfigured Christian rituals in all kinds of ways. Baptisms solemnized by extemporaneous prayer bless mountainside retreat center lakes. The body and blood of Christ can take the form of rice cakes and plum wine where Asian heritage is deeply knit with eucharistic practice. Tonal language that no documenter of ancient liturgy knew makes clear what those elements signify. Revival services and concerts become new forms of Christian worship tradition. As we continue to preserve Christian tradition and participate in it, how will we also move within and extend its enduring and faithful motion?

Questions and Exercises

1. Tradition is in motion, and your leadership of worship contributes to the forward movement of tradition. Are we moving Christian worship into the future? Or are we merely repeating what you have inherited from the past?

2. Tradition has been multi-linear, multicultural, and intercultural from the beginning. No one tradition then is superior to any others or has authority over them. In our leadership, design, and implementation of worship, what would it look like to lead with liturgical hospitality and humility?

3. Tradition encompasses more than our particular denomination's past. Therefore, when we look for historical liturgical resources, the availability of liturgical resources is panoramic with respect to race, gender, ethnicity, political leaning, socioeconomic class, sexuality, geography, confession, and more. How would our worship leadership grow if we referenced the array of how liturgy has taken shape across traditions on a regular basis, and not only as tokens of insight for occasional services where we wanted to highlight a particular identity politic?

THE INSCRUTABLE PREFERENCE FOR TWO PATTERNS

Protestant Christian worship in the United States tends to follow two patterns. One pattern is a sequence of three movements; the other comprises four. The three-movement pattern, found most often in nondenominational, charismatic, and evangelical congregations, consists of (1) extended congregational song or instrumental music; (2) a proclamation that can last thirty to forty-five minutes or longer; and (3) a time of response consisting of more congregational song or instrumental music, congregational prayer, and acts of healing, prophecy, or other contemplative and charismatic actions that range from silent meditation to glossolalia sometimes accompanied by convulsing and bodily collapse, colloquially known as being "slain in the Spirit."[1] The fourfold pattern, more often seen in mainline Protestant congregations such as The United Methodist Church, the Evangelical Lutheran Church in America, the Presbyterian Church (USA), the Episcopal Church, the American Baptist churches, the United Church of Christ, the Christian Church (Disciples of Christ), Quakers (in its programmed worship), Reformed Church in America, and African Methodist Episcopal churches, consists of (1) gathering, (2) proclamation and response, (3) thanksgiving and Communion or response, and (4) sending forth. Across the United States, and the remaining world as well, Christian worship in Protestant churches follows one of the three- and fourfold movement patterns, or some variation of them. If, however, Christian worship glorifies a God of infinite love who offers new life to all of humanity, then there must be more possibilities for structuring Christian worship.

Gordon Lathrop, in *Holy Things*, maintains that the ordo—a historical way of understanding an elemental pattern for Christian worship, which Lathrop condenses into gathering around the waters of baptism, the word proclaimed, and the Lord's Supper—grows out of the earliest experiences of Christian worship and comes directly from the Bible.[2] Yet Christian worship in its most antique forms was often simpler, more flexible, and open to interpretation.

In *The Earliest History of the Christian Gathering*, Valeriy A. Alikin expands scholarship of early Christian gatherings by asserting that they grew out of more than Jewish antecedents or originary Christian texts and theology.[3] The larger context of Greco-Roman banqueting practices influenced the character and activities of early Christian assemblies. Following scholars such as M. Klinghardt, H. J. de Jonge, and D. Smith, Alikin sees two practices from Greco-Roman culture consistently suturing early Christian gatherings as they standardize in the fourth and fifth centuries.[4] The two practices are (1) that of a supper (*deipnon,* which would be solemnized as Eucharist by Christians) and (2) a symposium (*symposion,* a time of libation and socializing following the main meal).

Alikin explains how the *deipnon* and *symposion* followed a pattern of customs. He describes how mostly male guests to a Greco-Roman deipnon would typically take a bath prior to their arrival at the host's home. The class-based patriarchy of Greco-Roman culture more often limited attendance to *deipnoi* to men. Only a few Roman women were sometimes granted permission to join formal meals. Servants would wash the feet of guests. Then guests would recline, wash their hands in shared and passed bowls, and eat three courses by hand: (1) vegetables, herbs, and olives; (2) either fowl and fish, or both; and (3) cheese, various fruits, and cakes.[5] Drinking mostly followed the main meal in the classical period for the Greeks. Wine was served throughout during the Hellenistic period, even as an aperitif. Eating and drinking became so interwoven in Hellenistic and Roman times that distinguishing when the *deipnon* concluded and the *symposion* began became unclear.

A toast to a deity who was considered the patron of the event or association usually marked the commencement of the *symposion.* Instructions then followed regarding when and how much guests should drink unless other directions for autonomous drinking had been given before the meal. Activities such as conversations, speeches, poetry recitations, literature readings, music making, dancing, and perhaps sexual services from female prostitutes also filled the *symposion.* Even in the midst of such celebration without inhibition, Alikin writes that the associations and their periodic meal celebrations provided male and female members a social fabric broader than the family and more intimate than the polis.[6]

Christian gatherings, which strove to forge family unrelated by blood with the love of God, appropriated the *deipnon* during the first three centuries into a Sunday-evening eucharistic meal with prayers beforehand and afterward. Prayers continued into the second half of the gathering, where the reading of scriptures, as well as singing and music making, prophesying, teaching, making acclamations, and other ritual actions occurred, all of which for Alikin present sacred analogues to the practices of the *symposion.* While Lathrop roots the Christian *ordo* in scripture, Alikin provides another live influence in her depiction of the social club and festive vibe of *deipnon* and *symposion* gatherings from Greco-Roman antiquity. Her research plays an important part in filling out the history of how we have come to pattern Christian worship the way that we do. She shows that what would later be identified as a biblically based *ordo* championed by thinkers such as Lathrop also had traces of libertine banqueting practices of Greco-Roman feasting culture. The solemnization of the *deipnon* and *symposion* is not, however, an uncritical adoption. Scandalous practices are left behind and replaced with devotional acts of obedience and freedom guided by the Holy Spirit and the discernment of the great cloud of witnesses. The roots of Christian worship are therefore scriptural and cultural, sacred and secular, and still growing in ways that seek the will of God with regard to receiving and resisting the winds of cultural change.

Realizing that the patterns of Christian worship have formed as a result of theological synergy between the reverent and irreverent helps us destabilize rigidity toward insisting upon particular patterns of worship as particularly of God. It helps us see how much was learned, absorbed, and blessed from outside Christianity in order to develop tried-and-true ways of glorifying God together. The openness and willingness of early Christian communities not only to engage with outside influences but also to take them on as capable of manifesting conditions for the praise and love of God helps us rethink possibilities for structuring Christian worship now and into the future. We can release ourselves from any orthodoxies associated with frameworks of worship. Instead, we begin to see any opportunity to pattern worship as an opportunity to design and plan with the recognition about which Rowan Williams shared in an address at Trinity Episcopal Church in New Haven, Connecticut, on June 21, 2018, that "the time of liturgy is, fundamentally, the time of God's healing engagement with humanity, the time of scriptural narrative, above all the time of the paschal mystery."[7]

In other words, deeper understanding about the varied metabolic processes at work in the formation of patterned worship from the past gives us a more substantial way of structuring worship with an eye toward God's future. What Williams suggests is that when liturgy happens, it does far more than merely preserve, transmit, or organize our worship practices with respect to idealized and historical understandings of how Christian worship should take place. Liturgical time ultimately points us to the mystery of God's future. If what he states rings true, why do we limit such incomprehensible spiritual, embodied, and divine healing and joy for the most part to two three- and fourfold patterns of worship? And what would it look like to reclaim tradition and innovation in the historical adaptation and potential liturgical flexibility going forward in the simplicity of the *deipnon* and *symposion* structure? If the heavens proclaim the glory of God and every day and night communicate theological knowledge, surely two patterns of worship and their well-worn alternatives do not exhaust the possibilities for Christian worship of the infinite God.

There are of course other variations of worship services that do not resemble the three- and four-movement patterns. Here are some examples:

Jazz Vespers

Taize worship

Prayer Services

Services of Healing or Anointing of the Sick

Love (Agape) Feasts

Stations of the Cross

Testimony Services

Emergent Church variations on rituals and rites

House Church worship

Questions and Exercises

1. If Alikin is right that the sequence of the *deipnon* and *symposion* provides ground for the earliest of Christian gatherings, how might you reconfigure worship with a more streamlined approach? Services such as the Agape Feast, an ancient Christian gathering believed by scholars to be linked to the Eucharist, but later celebrated as a separate meal of reconciliation and fellowship, and its fruit such as "Dinner Church" already exist. But what would it entail to begin with an inviting and accessible meal where the unfolding

of etiquette and the use of ingredients celebrate unifying and cross-cultural power of the Holy Spirit, and then conclude with interactive liturgical celebration and libation?

2. Or, how might you boil down your pattern of worship to just two parts and then build the order from there? What might be gained by a simpler and less-encumbered approach to the formation of worship?

3. Where might you find room in the natural rhythm of your church's worship life to begin to explore worship patterns outside of the three- and fourfold patterns? Imagine using experiences of the community (testimony services), creative and artistic expression (celebration of God through the arts), and special occasions (i.e., weddings) as an opportunity to introduce new patterns and rhythms into your community.

SCRIPTURE

Scripture provides a foundation for Christian worship. Yet it leaves room for the work of the Holy Spirit to move among worship leaders in any given age as they navigate how to lead worship for their context and time. As a canon of diverse writings translated from the originary languages of Hebrew, Greek, and Aramaic, the liturgical ground it offers is as dizzying and complex as life itself is in any age. Furthermore, while scripture provides a foundation for worship, it does not detail how Christian worship leadership should take place. In Acts, an account of how the earliest Christian churches worshipped, we know that followers of Jesus prayed, proclaimed messages of the gospel, spoke in tongues as gifted by the Holy Spirit, baptized, gave away possessions, held things in common, broke bread, healed, anointed, read and taught from the scriptures, praised God, buried the dead, gave alms, prophesied, and saw light and had visions, for example. But we do not know how. Acts is not an instruction manual or guidebook for worship. Some scholars believe the writing is an idealized account.

In the Old Testament, we read about an array of individual and cultic practices that continue to shape how we understand personal and collective piety, sacrifice, and praise today. Language from Deuteronomy 6:4-5 and selections from the Psalter are ready-made prayers. We baptize because the Gospels tell us that Jesus was baptized, and connect baptism to the ritual washings of repentance practiced by the Israelites. Yet as Maxwell E. Johnson writes, where John the Baptist learned to baptize or how he was authorized, we do not know.[1] We celebrate the Lord's Supper because narratives across the New Testament describe how Jesus first hosted the meal with his disciples, and its establishment is rooted in the celebration of Passover according to the Bible. However, scholars have not been able to verify the link.[2] Acts recounts sabbath observances, prayer, revelation, glossolalia, proclamations, signs and wonders, praise, breaking bread, acts of giving alms and dispossession, teaching inside and outside of the temple, individual and corporate prayer, silence, confession, repentance, burials, baptism, the laying on of hands, healing and other miracles, fasting, hymn singing, prophesying, visions, and conversion first taking place with Jews and then opening expansively to Gentiles. Yet there are almost no instructions for the biblical actions of worship. Even the Lord's Prayer found in Matthew 6:9-13 and Luke 11:2-4 does not exactly match what has become standardized in churches now. Directions for other practices that we might identify as worship found in chapters such as Matthew 5 and 6, Luke 11 and 12, 1 Corinthians 14, and elsewhere in the New Testament leave a lot of room for interpretation. And some of the restrictions regarding the participation of women, for example, need reinterpretation.

While Scripture authorizes so much of Christian worship today, it does not capture the possibilities for expression of individual and collective devotion to God. As much as it introduces us to the landscape of worship practices that have evolved into how we worship now, it sometimes even limits our vision for what faithful worship can be.

Appealing to scripture to inspire dynamic Christian worship leadership, therefore, also requires inspiration from our imaginations given to us by God. Alongside reading scripture, we must discern what is needed for our time and place in particular. We must also look and listen for how God is speaking to us now and in the lives of others and within the reverberations of creation at large. Fusing the needs of our current era, the flashes of revelation given to us by God in the world, and what we read in scripture helps us generate empowering acts of worship custom made for the people we serve.

Questions and Exercises

1. List the biblical passages to which you refer most often in worship.

2. How have they already been altered for use in your context? For example, has the lectionary shortened or compressed them? How close or far do you think they are from the originating translations of Greek, Hebrew, and Aramaic?

3. What would it require to hear, learn, and read those texts and indeed the entire canon in Greek, Hebrew, and Aramaic in worship?

4. What are other passages in the Bible or your favorite selections that could inspire meaningful worship? How would you use them in conversation with what you see the world needing and with respect to what you see God doing in the world to offer dynamic forms of worship?

OTHER SACRED TEXTS

From biblical times until now, countless other traditions have not only existed alongside Judaism and Christianity, they have influenced them as well. Stories such as the creation of all people, creatures, flora, fauna, and things; the births of Ishmael to Hagar and Isaac to Sarah in Genesis; the long line of David linked to Jesus in Matthew; and the culmination of all nations, tribes, people, and languages that praise the Lamb of Revelation suggest that the God in which we believe is a God of many traditions. Moreover, Mark Smith details how the very ways in which God has been conceived and articulated have their origins in the language and phrasing of Egyptian, Ugarit, Levantine, Mesopotamian, and other Near Eastern cultures.[1] In other words, influences that we might consider polytheistic or far from Judeo-Christian traditions are in fact integral to how we think and speak about God. Determining what makes a text sacred is blurrier and has more historical and present-day twists and turns than we might at first expect. The sacred is crafted over time by human calling and ingenuity and not merely given.

Modern translations like Eugene Peterson's *The Message* incorporates twentieth-century language to make scripture come alive for certain hearers. The Common English Bible uses language readable according to the most general level of literacy in the United States. Robert Alter's Hebrew Bible translation and commentary renders the ancient text with poetic power. Under the leadership of Martha Simmons, the African American Lectionary project reframed how we read biblical texts and understand them within what constitutes holy time with honor to the vast gifts of African American culture.[2] Drawing inspiration from sacred texts and people outside of the biblical canon continues as an option to strengthen the leadership of Christian worship today.

Questions and Exercises

1. Spend ten minutes a day reading a copy of the Qur'an, the Yogasutras, the Upanishads, the Vedas, or another collection of sacred writings. As you become more familiar with these kinds of writings, ask how the knowledge they present can enliven your Christian understandings of God.

2. For example, if in worship you were to pair a biblical reading with a reading from a sacred text of another tradition, how might that kind of comparison and contrast spoken aloud in public worship illuminate differences in how God has been understood across traditions and bring into relief the distinctive ways that Christianity portrays God?

3. Read an Old Testament passage in worship as an Abrahamic text, as sacred text shared between Judaism, Islam, and Christianity. For example, compare the story of Joseph from Genesis 37–45 in the Hebrew Bible with the story of Yusuf (Joseph) in the Qur'an 12:1-102. How do the differences between the narratives bring a different kind of synergy to the interpretation of scripture for worship?

4. What texts not readily considered theological or religious are sacred to you? Spoken word or poetry might be examples. What is it about those readings that articulated something of the divine or who we are in God? Are there ways that you could incorporate those texts in worship alongside biblical passages or as testimonies that stand on their own?

5. In addition to the legible, what cultural artifacts might constitute living or three-dimensional "sacred texts"? For example, if historically we know that the basilica was a public hall long before its form was used as a template for sanctuaries and that clergy vestments are patterned after imperial robes, what other artifacts might we adopt from culture and solemnize in order to widen our imagination or express something crucial about who we are in God and who God is for us? Could a hoodie become a relic of the Holy Spirit sighing too deep for words or a tattoo bear witness to the wounds of Christ?

INTERRELIGIOUS DIALOGUE

Interreligious dialogue in the context of *A Worship Workbook* describes interactivity between Christian worship and any other mode of belief, even modes of belief prior to the existence of Christian worship. For example, the Bible is shaped by a myriad of sources that predate not only Jesus of Nazareth but also the formation of Israelite beliefs. Pre-biblical Ugaritic and Mesopotamian conceptions of God influence and inform Hebrew Bible understandings of *Yahweh*. Ugarit was an ancient port city in Northern Syria. Mesopotamia, in Greek meaning "between two rivers," was an ancient region along the Tigris-Euphrates River system in land that now corresponds to Iraq, and parts of Iran, Syria, and Turkey. The people of Ugarit and Mesopotamia were not Israelites. What we call interreligious dialogue has been a part of worship from before the beginning, described in Genesis. Yet even as the array of Israelite belief became identifiable as Judaism, it never achieved consensus. Difference has always been a part of Jewish belief.

Christianity itself is a divergent form of Jewish belief. John the Baptist, Jesus, the disciples, Paul, Mary Magdalene, Mary the mother of James, and Salome were all Jewish. While Christian churches today may not have many Jewish adherents, every Christian worshipping community today has different modes of belief operating within them as well as neighbors who believe differently from the way they do and with whom they can dialogue. Often, the neighbors of differing beliefs are linked to a shared biblical history, one that begins with a biblical bond shared through Abraham by modern Judaism, Christianity, and Islam. Today, each of those traditions has blossomed into further expressions.

Contemporary Judaism is Ashkenazi or Sephardic. Ashkenaz was first applied in the Middle Ages as an identifier to diasporic Jews living along the Rhine River in Northern France and Western Germany.[1] It has four major branches: Orthodox, Conservative, Reconstruction, and Reform, each with various shoots that differentiate among themselves such as Renewal, Humanistic, and Transdenominational. Sephardic Jews are descendants of Jews who were expelled from Spain or Portugal as a result of the 1492 expulsion when Jews were driven out of those countries by decree from the Catholic monarchs King Ferdinand II of Aragon and Queen Isabella I of Castile. *Sephardic* comes from *Sepharad*, the biblical Hebrew word for Spain.[2]

Christianity has three major branches: Catholic, Orthodox, and Protestant. Orthodoxy splits into two primary families. Both Catholicism and Orthodoxy claim origins to Jesus of Nazareth and his apostles. Yet the schism that separated the Orthodox Church from Catholicism can be traced back to the year 1054 and disagreements that included differences regarding pneumatology, sacramental practices, and ecclesial authority between Greek East and Latin West churches. Protestantism began in Germany in 1517. Islam has two principal branches: Sunni and Shia. Sunnis compose 90 percent of the world's Muslims. The name derives from "Ahl al-Sunnah," or "People of the Tradition."[3] "The Tradition" refers to interpretations of teachings and practices based upon the revelation received by Muhammed. Sunnis hold fast to Hanafi, Maliki, Shafi'I, and Hanbali thoughts. Shias derive their name from "Shiat Ali" or the "Party of Ali."[4] Shias see Ali as the rightful successor to the prophet Muhammed following his death in 632. Shias have a majority population in Iran, Iraq, Bahrain, Azerbaijan, and by some counts, Yemen. Shias divide into the Twelvers, Isma'ilis, Zaydis, and Bohras with the majority belonging to the Twelvers. Sufism, or tasawwuf in Arabic, is a mystical form of Islam, prioritizing interior spirituality and closeness with God, as well as the cherishing of peace, love, and tolerance. Sunnis and Shias have adopted some practices and thoughts of Sufism.[5]

We encourage readers to learn more about the traditions discussed here as touchpoints for embracing interreligious dialogue. For our purposes, our intention is not to dive into detail. Rather, we simply want to show how fundamental and how kaleidoscopic interreligious dialogue is to the formation and continuation of Christian worship. We have introduced facets of the wide and rich diversity of Abrahamic faiths in order to show how interreligious dialogue envelops and informs Christian belief. We could have also discussed so many more traditions. In any case, we hope the reader has caught a glimpse as to how Christian worship has been, is already, and will continue to be engaged in interreligious dialogue.

Questions and Exercises

1. Visit a congregation or community of faith outside of the Christian tradition and invite those whom you serve in worship leadership to join you. What did you experience? Was it a one-time field trip? Or will it influence the way that you shape Christian worship from now onward and therefore require touching base again?

2. What would it look like to make visiting a non-Christian tradition a regular habit of weekly worship? Visiting online may make such liturgical exploration more accessible. How could experience of worship from another religious tradition influence worship in our home setting of Christian worship?

3. Maybe there are members of your congregation with extended family from different religious traditions. What would it look like to invite those family members into a time of testimony during worship? How would that expand the sense of hospitality within

worship and also perhaps lead to new insights regarding the wideness of human imagination for God?

4. How would inviting other religious leaders into the pulpit on a Sunday morning foster positive theological dialogue and expanded conversations about how humans have imagined who God is and who they are in God?

5. If expertise is needed to clarify the complexities of interreligious dialogue, how might educators from a local college or a local high school (someone who instructs world religions, for example) or even co-workers of other religions be invited as guest speakers during a worship service, not as token representatives of differing belief, but as neighbors who offer wider theological conversation and knowledge?

THE SACRAMENTS

Other texts delve into intricate discussion regarding the meaning of the sacraments or sacramental theology. Here, we emphasize practical recommendations for making sacramental practice as accessible and as hospitable as possible.

The list of sacraments can include up to seven: (1) baptism, (2) confirmation, (3) Eucharist, (4) penance, (5) extreme unction or anointing of the sick, (6) marriage, and (7) ordination. As Protestant authors writing ecumenically, baptism and the Eucharist (also known as the Lord's Supper and Communion) anchor the following discussion of sacramental practices across Christian congregations.

THE SACRAMENTS—BAPTISM

Baptism is *the* rite of initiation into Christian churches. It is practiced everywhere communities of faith celebrate the grace of God. Its familiarity, however, has unknown roots. The enigmatic origins of the practice open the possibilities for ongoing interpretive variation as to how baptisms happen.

How John became a baptizer or where he developed his baptismal practices remains a mystery. The Gospel of John does not mention Jesus being baptized. It does, however, mention him baptizing others (John 3:22, 26, 4:1; but cf. 4:2).[1] The biblical evidence for baptism, for liturgical historian Paul Bradshaw, brings the question if the Christian adoption of baptism began with Jesus or after his resurrection.

When the baptism of infants began also remains a mystery. The first undisputed reference is one from Tertullian in the third century, according to Bradshaw. Tertullian disapproves of the practice. Baptizing children in the earliest centuries seemed mostly concerned with providing fire insurance for the child. Augustine thought that newborns were without sin. Yet they inherited original sin from Adam and therefore needed baptism as much as an adult. Augustine himself was not baptized until he was an adult. Many people in antiquity delayed baptism as long as possible to ensure all of their sins were washed away.

The Greek word *baptizein* means "dipping." Whether by dipping, dripping, or dunking, Bradshaw also raises suspicion regarding immersion in water as a universal practice in Christian rites of initiation from the beginning. There was likely some kind of ritual dialogue (and maybe catechesis) prior to immersion.[2] Yet total immersion would not have been possible in domestic baths. According to Bradshaw, some early baptizands stood in shallow fonts and had water poured over them. Immersion into water was achieved in different ways as it continues to be now. The practices were pluriform. Today, it therefore makes sense that the action of performing a baptism would continue to vary with considerable degree. The argument that one method of applying the baptismal water is superior over another is spurious if we appeal to the long history of baptism.

Paul tells us that we are baptized into the death and new life of Jesus (Romans 6:3-4). Finding symmetry in the watery chaos out of which God created the world in Genesis, Rowan Williams writes that in baptism we are in touch with the chaos in our own lives, and we surface into the creative act of God's love and grace in our lives.[3] The Holy Spirit embraces us in delight and dedicated transformation made possible by faithfulness to God and God's church. We agree with the theological interpretations of baptism from Paul and Williams. Yet we also suggest that the newness of Christ's life has informed baptismal practices following his own baptism from the very beginning. Baptismal practices were invented as much as they were transmitted. They can remain novel in the variety of their expression now. Furthermore, the creative act of God's love and grace in our lives has continually shaped baptismal practice over millennia from start to finish, from the commencement of the rite before water touches anything or anyone to the drying of consecrated heads and bodies. [The divine creativity inherent in baptism should continue to inform theologically profound interpretations and a dynamic multiplicity of baptismal practices as we extend welcome and cherish embracing neighbors, strangers, and enemies as family in the name of Christ now from our time into the future.]

Questions and Exercises

1. If immersion happened in different ways, what are the advantages of baptizing with different types of water, still and living, fresh and salt, and with different kinds of gestures, dripping or submerging?

2. In addition to experimenting with using different kinds of water and ways to administer it, how might other sensorial elements present at a baptismal service lend themselves to modification in order to drive symbolic meaning, such as the lighting to evoke plunging into the darkness and chaos of life before surfacing into the light of Christ and the Holy Spirit, fragrance with the use of incense or scented candles that are hypoallergenic, varying arrangements of background music, paraments and other pulpit area, altar, and stage ornamentation, and so forth?

3. If baptism is a rite of initiation into an ecclesial community, should baptisms happen more often collectively, that is, with more than one family, and especially shared between folks who are not related by blood to one another to emphasize joining into the family of God?

4. If gathering a congregation is not possible for a baptism, what are ways to share a baptism that occur through a private pastoral visit? Live streaming is one. Yet perhaps planning a recording could be another so that the video of the baptism could be used again as testimony within a service.

5. If baptism must be contactless, how might a medical professional assist in a hospital or home setting with a baptism?

6. Access to clean water is a pressing problem also related to income inequality and racial prejudice as well as a host of other social factors. How might the liturgy or speech said during a baptism also include proclamations about how God desires us to care for the waters by which we celebrate initiation into the body of Christ? What can we say and what gestures or accompanying rituals might we also undertake in order to convey that we are incomplete as a body of Christ unless water everywhere, the universal element of Christian baptism, is clean and safe for everyone, including the most vulnerable and disenfranchised?

THE SACRAMENTS—EUCHARIST

Whether we call it Communion, the Lord's Supper, or the Eucharist, the Eucharist invites participants of Christian worship everywhere to gather around a common table to share gifts of bread and wine or grape juice that celebrate new life in Jesus Christ. (We have chosen Eucharist here as a nod to the original Greek translation of the rite from *eucharistia* [thanksgiving].) Across Protestant congregations, eucharistic practice varies widely from fine-tuned liturgies found in prayer books to makeshift tableaus where crackers and tiny cups of juice are loosely arranged on bar tables while a band plays ethereal or popular music. Sometimes, the formal and casual mix like popular-music infused celebrations of the Lord's Supper such as U2charist or Beyoncé Mass services. In other sacramental occasions, the Eucharist transcends space and time, with presiding happening in one location and receiving in another, such as the comfort of one's home. However we observe the Lord's Supper, patterns of eucharistic worship now grow out of wide diversity at the very beginning. The initial mysterious, varied, and innovative practices of eucharistic worship provide a vanishing point to celebrate Communion as an open table with flexibility in choice and distribution of the elements for the sake of wide welcome.

Narratives from Matthew 26:17-30; Mark 14:12-26; Luke 22:7-38; and 1 Corinthians 11:23-34 anchor eucharistic practice. Yet Paul Bradshaw asserts that the New Testament likely did not influence eucharistic practice authoritatively until the third century. It took a couple of centuries for the reception of the writings to move from apostolic writings to holy scripture.[1] Early texts such as the first-century Didache, The Teaching of the Twelve, which some scholars believe may be contemporary with the Gospels, do not describe the bread and wine in what appears to be a eucharistic meal as the body and blood of Christ. Neither is there an association of the meal as a Last Supper. The elements are instead described as spiritual food and drink.

The prayers in the Didache bear witness to a Jesus who brings "life, knowledge, and eternal life."[2] Emphasis upon the sacrificial and atoning death of Jesus is absent. Second-century writing from Ignatius describes the bread as "flesh" of Jesus instead of "body." Bradshaw suggests that this difference places the Ignatian eucharistic approach more in line with the Gospel of John instead of the Synoptics and Paul.[3] Notably, the Gospel of John does not include a eucharistic narrative. John 6 tells a miraculous feeding story where a crowd is satiated with five barley loaves and two fish from a young boy.

The Synoptic Gospels coincide the Last Supper with Passover. John's Gospel portrays a foot washing prior to Passover. Paul does not associate his account of the meal with Passover. Only he and the Synoptic Gospels position the meal as a last supper. Taking Bradshaw's findings that disentangle the Eucharist from Synoptic influence along with other historical reasons not detailed here, Bradshaw surmises that the first couple of centuries of eucharistic practice were more influenced by Johannine and selected Pauline understandings of the meal as a meal of life in Christ where the hungry are fed with food from God, not an observance especially aligned with Passover or one necessarily located at first as a last supper with the disciples prior to the death of Jesus. Therefore, the automatic and prevalent associations of the Eucharist primarily as a paschal meal focused upon the sacrifice of Jesus may overlook historical considerations that would help us also to view the meal as one of sharing life in Christ and feeding the hungry with the substance of God.

What we want readers to consider is how if the earliest celebrations of the Eucharist were more grounded in feeding the hungry and celebrating life in Christ, then any occasion of Communion ought to welcome and serve all those who hunger after the mercy and love of God. Disciples who deserted and betrayed Jesus were present at the Lord's Supper presented in the Gospels. Therefore, we recommend an open table practice for Eucharist at all times. By open table, we mean a table open to anyone. Leaders of worship also ought to adjust accordingly, in terms of approaching selection of the elements, consecration of them, and the fraction with flexibility, so that the Lord's Supper is made accessible and available to all. For example, a worship leader should be encouraged to host the Lord's Supper online.[4] As Teresa Berger writes, Claire of Assisi envisioned the Mass and all of its participants, although she could not be present physically due to illness.[5] The Eucharist also brings together communicants or participants who may otherwise distance themselves from one another intentionally and unintentionally in everyday life. The breaking of the bread and sharing of the wine paradoxically invites people of God into a unifying ritual that welcomes the fullness and brokenness of our lives. May we continue to envision and enact embracing forms of celebrating Communion.

When I was a pastor in England, I was asked not to preside or preach at Christmas Eve and Christmas Day services because I used the word *shit* during a sermon for a confirmation service. Inspired by Tony Campolo using the same vocabulary at Wheaton College to describe folks "not giving a shit" that thirty thousand children starve at night and the irony that more people would be offended by his use of profanity than so many children going hungry.[6] My sermonic variation deployed the word to talk about the resilience of a youth deciding to be confirmed in our church even though he was dying of a muscular degenerative disease. He had gone through "a lot of shit" and yet still wanted to be a part of God's family. Wasn't that an amazing withness of God? In any case, without any ministerial commitments for Christmas, I decided to offer Christmas Eve Communion in a local pub. Little did I realize that Christmas Eve in the English town where I served was like New Year's Eve. It was a massive miscalculation. A packed crowd reveled like there was no tomorrow. Just before midnight, the televisions and music were turned off and silenced. I was handed a microphone to preside at a makeshift altar in the middle of a balconied bar as large as a basketball court with two barmaids at my side as co-celebrants. Some parishioners came in support and sat on stools nervously whispering among themselves. A few guests heckled me as a I explained the tradition of midnight Communion. Yet eventually, every patron lined up to receive the body and blood of Christ. It was a miraculous experience of seeing just how wild, warm, fun, hungry, and thirsty the people of God are.[7]

Questions and Exercises

1. If the Eucharist as we know it is the result of all kinds of practices coming into standardized formation, how might that encourage us to be open with how we celebrate the Lord's Supper? How could the resources of other traditions inform our Table practices? Understanding how fluid the very beginnings of the Eucharist were helps us to also practice more flexibility in terms of how we share Communion. It prevents us from snubbing our noses at practices that we do not think are liturgically correct. Maybe online Communion isn't such a bad thing.

2. Even if the Eucharist was a last supper, how does the presence of Judas and Peter, disciples who would betray Jesus, compel us to see that even those whom we might consider to be the worst of sinners are welcome at the Table of God?

3. What does it mean for the Eucharist to invite our full selves (flawed and all) to the Table? How does it make us imagine who is welcome, and how we come to the Table? How does it even call us to reimagine who is in leadership at the Table?

4. Even if the Eucharist was a Passover meal, how does its Jewish association help us rethink how Communion can also be a site of interreligious and interfaith eating and drinking?

5. If the Eucharist in its earliest iterations was a meal celebrating abundant and everlasting life in Christ for the hungry, how can we orient our celebrations of Communion to serve as banquets for the physically and spiritually hungry?

6. How might prerecorded and live video exchange, liturgies sent by attachment or shared live, and even connection to members of other churches not bound by the immediate geographical location of the church, add to a eucharistic celebration online? If Eucharist

must be contactless, how might a medical professional assist in a hospital or home setting with a Eucharist?

7. If you have celebrated the Lord's Supper online, what did you learn from the experience, not just in terms of ritual practice, but also with regard to sacramental theology? Did you discover something new about the meaning of the supper by celebrating it online? Or, did you feel as if you were mostly improvising and making the most of a bad situation? What would you do differently moving forward? Would you make the ritual more intimate? How might youth or digitally savvy parishioners or colleagues help make the broadcasting technology not only a means of transmitting the celebration of the Lord's Supper? How might the technology itself evoke and represent the sacramental?

Chapter 11
PREACHING

Preaching is itself an act of worship and happens most frequently within the context of worship. Yet because homiletics, or the research and teaching of preaching, is a freestanding discipline with separate guild conversations, we will not aim in this chapter to provide summative or comprehensive advice regarding the art of preaching. For that we recommend *A Sermon Workbook*.[1] Instead, we want to offer in no particular order a set of recommendations for preaching that we believe would benefit preachers across ecclesial and cultural contexts, and that still seem nascent as widely practiced customs.

The first recommendation is to root Christian preaching in prayer. If preaching aims to spread the love of God and neighbor through proclamation, then we must first connect to God directly, not just through sacred text that mediates who God is for us. By rooting preaching in prayer, we are continuing the foundational reliance upon revelation and prayer that the earliest preachers introduced into antique house churches.

In the book *From Prophecy to Preaching*, Alistair Stewart-Sykes offers a prehistory of Christian preaching prior to the third century.[2] In the first two centuries, households hosted Christian worship. Stewart-Sykes suggests that in those homes, proclamation happened *in seriatim*, in a sequence, and perhaps around a table. Multiple speakers shared prophetic utterances they claimed to be given by God, one after the other. Then the assembly would enter *diakrisis*, a conversation where they would check what they heard with a scroll of scripture, maybe, for example, from Isaiah. They would judge, interpret, and when deemed appropriate, apply what was spoken. Over centuries, as household Christian worship evolved into a public hall like the basilica, what was at first a group of proclaimers in the murky origins of Christian preaching became collapsed into one preacher, a presiding bishop. The gathering table became an altar for the Eucharist. Words that began in revelation and then were checked with sacred text were derived in the opposite direction. Exegesis or the interpretation of scripture preceded proclamation. We see this reversal as early as the third century in Origen, who writes the first known commentary. The original communal dialogue of Christian proclamation becomes a monologue of preaching.

Today, preaching happens in a variety of ways, and there are long traditions of call-and-response that share a family resemblance to the earliest *diakrisis* of Christian preaching. What we want to especially highlight from Stewart-Sykes is his insistence that the earliest proclaimers relied first upon revelation or, more simply put, prayer. Though preaching is taught mostly as beginning with the interpretation of scripture, it would be nothing without prayer.

In his 2016 Beecher Lecture, *The End of Preaching*, Thomas H. Troeger constellates his remarks around a quotation from George Herbert's collection of sacred poems, *The Temple*.[3] Herbert was a seventeenth-century Welsh-born Anglican priest, and he has been canonized as one of the greatest Christian poets in the English language. He also lyricized in Latin and Greek. Troeger quotes a simple but striking line from Herbert, "Resort to sermons, but to prayers most: praying's the end of preaching."[4] For Troeger, Herbert's line is a reminder that preaching cultivates the devotional life of the congregation within a range of prayer. For example, preaching moves a congregation to adoration, confession, supplication, intercession, thanksgiving, and to lament. But the link we want to highlight between Troeger and the historical research of Stewart-Sykes is how prayer is both the beginning and the end of preaching.

Prayer, as we are referring to it, could also be seen as what homiletician Lisa Thompson in her book *Ingenuity* describes as the task of preachers to align themselves with preaching's greatest hopes—to move to what is most holy and true. Prayer, as we read it through Thompson, involves preachers looking beyond ourselves *to God* and in consultation with those devoted to God and even *those who aren't*, in order to discover flashes of Divine insight. A preacher might pray to God for help in interpreting a scriptural passage. But that is not what we mean here. What we are recommending is an engagement with prayer as elemental to the preaching practice. Listen for God first before reading any text or beginning any interpretation. See the image of God in others, look to them and their experience and knowledge as living iconography from which illuminated preparation for preaching can happen, as well as viewing pages for written truths. See the image of God even in enemies or those we despise or those we consider remote from Christian worship.

Why look to those who aren't devoted to God? Because Jesus calls us to love all, including those in whom we have no interest or might even consider our enemies. That kind of totalizing love helps us understand the work of God in every aspect of human life. In that way, our preaching can cast a panoramic vision of God's invitation and grace and mercy in the world. Importantly, preaching that depends upon prayer, or the revelation of God, doesn't mean jettisoning structure. Developing a robust theology of preaching requires structure. Our remaining recommendations appear in the questions and exercises below.

Questions and Exercises

1. Our most expansive prayer comes from the vision in Revelation of the countless multitude "from every nation, tribe, people, and language" praising the Lamb of God (Revelation 7:9). As you root your preaching in prayer, how will you ask for illumination from the Holy Spirit to preach regarding ecumenism, religious plurality, race, ethnicity, gender, sexuality, cognitive and physical ability, class, culture at large, and more?

2. In *A Sermon Workbook*, Troeger and Tubbs Tisdale recommend writing for the ear as being preferable for drafting a sermon. By "writing for the ear," they mean crafting your sermon manuscript with constant reflection about how it will be heard:

Short lines
are easier to follow.
Especially
if you're nervous.

Play around with this method.
Play with language.
Play with different ways of thinking.
Of seeing.
Of being.
Of communicating.

Kind of fun—
isn't it?
It will open you to the Spirit.
And your congregation too![5]

3. As you write for the ear, consider also applying your sermon to the following elements based upon Ted Smith's method for preaching without notes:

I. Preach one message. Can you boil it down to a single sentence?

II. Then outline the rest of your sermon in complete sentences. The sentences are prompts to expand in real time. Yet just as important, or even more important, think of the sentences as transition points in the sermon. They should read as a cohesive paragraph when put together.

III. For example, here is the current chapter outlined in complete sentence form:

    a. Preaching is rooted first in prayer, not exegesis.

    b. Alistair Stewart-Sykes shows us that the very first sermons began with direct revelation.

    c. Today, preaching happens in all kinds of ways.

    d. But it still begins in prayer (as Tom Troeger and Lisa Thompson emphasize now).

    e. Preaching rooted in prayer sees God's mercy across human life and the world.

IV. If you committed this outline to memory, do you think you could preach a sermon without notes? We believe so! You might still prepare by writing an entire manuscript in advance. But instead of committing a manuscript to memory, you would rehearse and digest it so that in the preaching moment, you could fly without a net by simply stating your outlined sentences verbatim at key points of transition, and elaborating upon each complete-sentence movement with extended proclamation that you have rehearsed beforehand or that you are crafting extemporaneously.[6]

Importantly, we do not think that preaching without notes or a manuscript is a superior form of Christian proclamation. Different occasions and different preaching dispositions will lend themselves to different methods. We encourage you to acquire as many preaching arrows in your quiver as you can so that you will be equipped for various homiletic targets.

4. The last recommendation we want to offer is to envision preaching as liturgical, catechetical, and missionary. Preaching is liturgical because it happens within the context of worship and often frames aspects of worship such as the sacraments of baptism and Communion. Or we might elaborate upon the wisdom of a hymn. It is catechetical because any sermon has the capacity to teach the assembly in facets of Christian faith. It is missionary because preaching can inspire service in the world that builds the *basileia* or reign of God. So, the next time that you preach, how will your prayer-based proclamation nurture collective doxology, theological learning, and service to every neighbor, including our enemies?

LANGUAGES OF LITURGY AND WORSHIP

At an address given to the North American Academy of Liturgy, Louis-Marie Chauvet admitted, "It's true: many words of our liturgies are worn out."[1] But even worn-out words help us worship God in Spirit and in truth and then live accordingly. As Geoffrey Wainwright writes, human life is marked by exteriority and interiority linked by the word. The word is thought (*logos endiathetos*) and announced or uttered (*logos prophorikos*).[2] In other words, worship can flourish, wither, or not do much of anything depending upon what we say and how we say it.

So, using different pronouns for God or finding other turns of phrase to reignite the fire of scriptural imagery is essential for effective worship that speaks to the range of humanity and touches upon the eternality of God. For example, Janet Walton writes:

> When a woman prays in the name of the community, she illustrates quite tangibly that no particular sound can be called "God's sound." When women offer their own perspectives on the living realities of faith, they reinforce the differences every person adds to interpretations of texts, symbols, and sacramental actions.[3]

The use of language expands our imagination for the Divine and how living a life of faith becomes comprehensible. In that way, Walton writes that feminist liturgy summons wonder.[4] Our language can lead the church to stretch its arms in welcome to anyone. It also entails much more than choosing appropriate pronouns. The use of sound liturgical language declares vistas of who we are in God and who God is for us.

Opening up our use of language now retrieves the verve found in Acts 2. There, the Holy Spirit gives divided tongues to a house of Iranians, Iraqis, Israelis, Turks, Asians, Egyptians, Libyans, Romans, both Jews and proselytes, Greeks, and Arabs. These are who the Parthians, Medes, Elamites, residents of Mesopotamia and Judea, Cappadocia, Pontus, Phrygia, Pamphylia, Cyrene, and Cretans are. With a symphony of languages, the Holy Spirit gusts through prejudice and xenophobia in Acts, resulting in miraculous communication that cuts across historical, political, geographical, theological, religious, economic, ethnic, racial, sexual, and generational lines. Pentecost is a geopolitical summit from two thousand years ago that would stun us even now. As an origin point for Christian worship, it challenges our complacency with mundane and monolingual liturgy today.

Moreover, polyphonic praise is our future too. Revelation points to a culmination of time and redemption of the entire creation declared by many languages praising God. Some might have concerns that in a monolingual congregation the introduction of another language might be too distracting. Yet what is important to remember is that even in a monolingual setting, we are already participating in multilingual worship. God's first language is not English, for example. Thus, we should always strive for openness to other tongues and to honor the original gifting of the Spirit and its incomprehensible benevolence of languages for the varied people of God.

I (Gerald) have been blessed to experience worship in many different languages. For example, the Boston Taiwanese Christian Church provided more exposure to Taiwanese American worship as it happens in a Taiwanese- and English-language setting. (I grew up in a Buddhist household.) Occasionally, I preach in settings that require translation or modification for those whose mother tongue is not English. For example, at Belmont United Methodist Church in Nashville, Tennessee, I was invited to preach in a service for The Golden Triangle Fellowship, a Southeast Asian congregation that also met alongside the larger historical congregation. My message was translated live into Karen, Thai, and Burmese. At the Taiwanese Presbyterian Church of Northern Jersey, my sermon was translated live into Taiwanese. At the Presbyterian Church in Leonia, New Jersey, my English sermon manuscript was printed and copied beforehand and made available on the morning of the service for distribution among the assembly so that Korean-, Japanese-, and Spanish-speaking parishioners could follow the preaching more easily. The way that the saints in all of those churches touched me with their multilingualism and accommodated my English displayed remarkable hospitality and congregational commitment to inclusivity in the name of God.

Questions and Exercises

1. How much of the language prayed, sung, read, spoken, and preached in your service(s) attempts to name God with more attention to the varied images of God found in the humanity created by God?

2. How much of the language prayed, sung, read, spoken, and preached in your service(s) is English? In what genres of worship do languages other than English appear? For example, is congregational song the worship practice most likely to incorporate a language other than English?

3. How much is the learning of other languages a part of your worship service(s)? Think about how much time each element of worship constitutes. Considering proportion, attempt to structure at least 50 percent or more of the service in a different language. Do you have participants of worship or neighbors who could be invited to participate in worship that are capable of instructing the assembly in a language other than English? What would it look like to incorporate the learning of another language as an exercise of prayer or praise and not a liturgical gimmick? What are the occasions when it would be easy to implement different languages and how could celebrating different liturgical languages become a regular congregational habit?

4. In some of our churches, we may already participate in multilingual worship on a regular basis. Or, we occasionally sing hymns, read scripture, pray, and even preach in different languages. What would it look like to decenter English as a regular vanguard practice of dynamic Christian worship? Reclaiming the originary multilingual miracle of Acts, how could we incorporate the sharing and learning of different languages in worship so that the word of God becomes more intelligible across a wider range of human speech?

5. Different translations of hymns and congregational songs are not hard to find. Different translations of the Bible are accessible. Prayers in other languages with transliteration of how to pronounce the words are often available through denominational offices or websites.

WEDDINGS

In the United States, weddings are more often celebrated outside of churches and by celebrants who are not professional ministers of the Christian faith.[1] Traditional Christian liturgies still determine or guide wedding services whether they take place in a destination or a congregation. Yet nonliturgical customs are more prevalent and more common forms of ritualizing such as sharing a first dance as newlyweds (90 percent of couples) or cutting the cake together (82 percent). Weddings also have a way of involving liturgical pageantry and invention that defy easy explanation or cohesion. Liturgy in a wedding is often more fluid and flexible, more akin to the antique definition of liturgy as broad service for the community. For example, guests might be asked to dress any way that they please and to sing together "Hey Jude" from the Beatles to kick off a ceremony in the aqua theater of the New York Aquarium that includes performing sea lions.[2] Weddings are also incredibly diverse occasions. Over half of all couples who marry differ in cultural background, especially with respect to religion, ethnicity, and where they call home. The regularity and welcome of diversity at a wedding likely eases the ask for participants in the ceremony to try something new. Planners, celebrants, family, friends, and crashers shrug and assume that whatever transpires during a wedding must have been envisioned or okayed by the couple.

Given the increased detachment from sanctuaries, their leaders, and the communities of faith who inhabit them, and the unpredictable permutations of ceremony pattern, and content, place, and parties we have chosen in the workbook to foreground how important it is to recognize the wedding as a blended rite for effective liturgical leadership. Recognizing the wedding as a blended rite in a Christian marriage may be obvious when, for example, a Chinese banquet accompanies a United Methodist wedding rite. Yet every wedding is a blended rite whether or not the liturgy changes because the brides, grooms, their families, friends, and crashers already bring cultural differences to the occasion. The pageantry and choreography of the ceremony already constitute the confluence of diverse backgrounds, whether or not they are explicitly Christian. Any presider at a wedding does well to discern cultural differences that do not immediately present themselves, and then to negotiate them with liturgical hospitality that indicates the graciousness of God in making possible enduring human love.

Even if the couple matches by way of cultural background such as gender and sexuality, and the planning and implementation of the service go relatively smoothly, it may be helpful to recall that the ancient history of the wedding is such that it was a state-sanctioned rite long before it was solemnized by the Christian church.[3] In other words, marriage as we know it in Christianity began with the joining of the secular to the sacred where the commitment of a couple to love each other exclusively for life was blessed in the name of God. It is perhaps one of the most visible and public ways churches meet communities to display how human love is sanctified by God. Therefore, we should not fear cultural changes such as the ratification of law making same-sex celebrations legal. As Willie Jennings says in his Acts Commentary, "Marriage folded into discipleship always becomes more than the work imagines, more than the state envisions, and more than those so enjoined understand."[4] Their love becomes the "site of God's outrageous joy."[5] If we follow the logic of Jennings, we should also see in every wedding, including weddings that may seem scandalous or sinful to some such as a same-sex marriage, as a coronation of surplus love with potential to bear witness to how radical and boundary-breaking the love of God can be, an instance of grace shining through law.

Questions and Exercises

1. What is the place in worship planning for a wedding in meeting the couple where they are? And when we understand that the social location of the couple is as much "where they are" as the actual requests regarding the pattern, content, and flow of the service, how can we as celebrants of weddings help the couple deeply knit aspects of their idiomatic senses of culture into a service that at its core is a celebration that God shares with everyone?

2. If wedding parties represent different religious traditions, how might a wedding ceremony also be an occasion to bear witness to interreligious worship that is meaningful and offered with integrity to the traditions involved?

3. Given that weddings bring together persons who represent a myriad of cultures and often include guests who rarely if ever attend church, how might a wedding service be structured as a service of evangelism bearing witness to the justice, peace, grace, and mercy of Jesus Christ?

4. The future of ritual ceremonies, such as weddings, will continue to evolve with heightened awareness for health and safety measures, become more intimate in-person occasions, and even continue the live digital engagement. How do these changes call for a new way of planning and leading weddings? How might the new ways of holding weddings offer creative opportunities for evangelism rooted in divine love?

FUNERALS

A funeral ultimately celebrates the promise of God's presence even at the point of death and the promise of new life in Christ. Among the repertoire of Christian services, a funeral service will typically incorporate fewer elements of liturgical creativity. Yet there are therapeutic dimensions that the liturgist must take seriously in addition to the transcendent and embodied claims regarding resurrection hope. In *Accompany Them with Singing*, Tom Long admits that pastors cannot make a funeral good. What he means is that while a presider may excel at the priestly functions of a funeral, the funeral is a service that all of those gathered enact. According to Long, it is "an ensemble performance," not "a pastoral soliloquy."[1] We are together mourning the dead and remembering the promises of new life given by Christ. Extending Long's notion of "ensemble performance," worship leaders must pastorally consider the needs of the mourners to honor the dead, including when requests or the situation at hand may challenge our presuppositions of what is liturgically appropriate. We must balance the needs of the grieving to mourn transitionally and psychologically with sound ritual and proclaimed address to questions of how we understand life and death in the context of worshipping a God who promises resurrection and new life.

It is important to note that by psychological and emotional needs, we do not at all recommend playing "armchair psychologist" or inappropriately moralizing to make a theological impact, meaning we should tend to the sorrow of the family and friends in a pastorally responsible and sensitive way.

The Reverend Sarah Mount Elewonini, Ph.D., a working United Methodist pastor and continuing education professor of working clergy, helps to elucidate the point. She notes that funerals, especially in the face of tragic deaths, are no time for preaching about how drugs are sinful, that suicide is a mortal sin without forgiveness, or that baptism is essential for salvation. None of these three claims can be warranted in an absolute way. Nor do they help spread the promise of justice, mercy, and new life in God.

Consider instead how Elewonini responds to a death from addiction:

When Timothy's mother arrived, her sister, parents, and the Holy Spirit entered my study with her. The family had a fifty-year-old, threadbare connection to our congregation. Yet I was immediately impressed with their strong, prayerful connection to God and one another.

At just thirty, Timothy Grillo-Feeney had lost his battle with opioid addiction on his grandfather's birthday. His family loved him fiercely, and, returning their love, Timothy struggled to remain hopeful about his future even hours before he died. His mother's deepest desire was that we make time for those who gathered to stitch together stories revealing that Timothy was *not* his addiction. Timothy was a wonderful, beloved child of God. Abundant potential, snuffed out. For a "non-church" family, their requests for hymns and prayers were remarkably thoughtful and apropos. So when they added "Over the Rainbow" to the list, though I was aware of the liturgical red flag, I didn't have the heart to say no.

Reflecting on the many ways in which symbols in *The Wizard of Oz* echo the pattern of the gospel I came to the conclusion that "over the rainbow" is another name for heaven, Zion, the promised land. Drawing many honest parallels between Timothy's life and the gospel I ended my sermon by proclaiming, "The heart of the Christian message is we don't have to wait to die to get to there. Through Jesus paradise is brought to us here. That's what 'Thy Kingdom come, thy will be done on earth as it is in heaven' means! Resurrection brings the other side of the rainbow to us."

We ended the service singing the beloved American anthem with my altered conclusion: "This home over the rainbow it is true! God's love is here, not just over the rainbow, embracing me and you."

At the time of this writing, the COVID-19 pandemic made it unsafe for funerals to happen at all, and in instances where they were able to happen, the funerals were a far cry from what we might have imagined as normal. In some cases, people were dying and buried alone; in other instances, only select family members of ten or fewer were permitted to be in attendance. What kind of ritualizing becomes possible when the very conditions for having a funeral are prohibited? We believe that even when gathering to mourn the dead and look to God for life in the face of death is prohibited, there are ways to honor the deceased, comfort the grieving, and proclaim the unfailing presence of the Holy Spirit with pastoral resolve and effectiveness.

Questions and Exercises

1. Recall the loss of a loved one in your life. If you have not experienced the death of a loved one, consider reading titles such as C. S. Lewis's *A Grief Observed*, Joan Didion's *The Year of Magical Thinking*, Leo Tolstoy's *The Death of Ivan Ilych*, and Joan Cacciatore's *Bearing the Unbearable*. How can mining the memories of your own feelings of loss and the insights shared by cogent authors help us build into funeral presiding a filigreed attention to the psychological demands present within the assembly of a funeral?

2. Conceive of the funeral service as one extended prayer before God. It relies upon existing customs, patterns, and language from denominational materials or resources online to express such theological power. It also demands skilled application of emotional intelligence and articulation of pastoral sensitivity from the presider. It looks toward the light of resurrection even in the face of inexplicable tragedy, unimaginable violence, or suicide, at every age. In preparation for any funeral service, how does each element in the service unify as prayer to honor, lament, plea, grieve, and comfort on behalf of the deceased and their mourners?

3. If the funeral service ultimately serves the living, how can you position your preaching and the liturgy with attention to emotional and psychological needs of the mourning as well as reminders of God's promises and invitations to those who grieve?

OTHER OCCASIONAL SERVICES

Christian worship is marked with a number of services and celebrations. In addition to weekly worship, weddings and funerals are perhaps the most familiar occasional services. But there are many more that fill the lives of congregations. Occasional services help turn an ecology of worship in any given context into a galaxy of proclamation, prayer, song, lament, ritual, and praise. Occasional services mark specific moments of the church community. They can take place during the weekly rhythm and order of worship. Or, they can bring the congregation together at special times and perhaps in special places to honor particular observances in the name of God that may or may not appear in the regular flow of liturgical time. Occasional services include, but are not limited to, either Children or Youth Sunday, or both; Men's Day; Women's Day; Black History Sundays (often marked in February); Martin Luther King Jr. worship service (generally held on the Sunday before national MLK Day); Coming Out and Solidarity Sundays; Asian North American Heritage, Latinx, Native American, Indigenous Peoples, and First Nations celebrations; Veteran's Day services; interfaith services; baccalaureate; Sundays that recognize the wide and incredible diversity of God's people; Taizé; lessons and carols; Stations of the Cross; foot washing; World Communion Sunday; church anniversaries; installation services for lay and ordained ministers, leaders, music directors, and teachers of the church; a love feast; blessing for the adoption of a child; the blessing of animals and homes; the consecration of musical instruments, liturgical items, and furnishings; and pastoral anniversaries. These services and more are all occasional services that fill out liturgical spaces not typically touched by the regular schedule of worship in any given community of faith, and they make worship filigreed and radiant with an array of holy light-sharing facets.

I (Gerald) once had a student who created a shared ritual to honor her divorce and re-marriage. She designed a service with a group of close friends where the central ritual consisted of wrapping porcelain tableware she had received from her first marriage in a blanket, breaking it together with friends on a shoreline, and then reconfiguring the shards into a tabletop mosaic that would be featured in the kitchen of her new home with her new partner. I found the intimacy, vulnerability, lament, hope, and redemption expressed in her service courageous. The ways that her invented ritual acknowledged the pain of divorce and the grace of finding a life partner again was theologically concrete and pastorally profound.

It would be impossible to name all of the current and potential occasional services that reach beyond customary ones such as weddings and funerals. What we want to recommend for you is to see occasional services not merely as a liturgical filler that checks boxes related to human diversity, social justice, sacred music genre, ecumenism, local ecclesial tradition, high holy days, and other pastoral and congregational considerations that the church feels compelled to address in worship. Rather, occasional services are worship events of revival that illuminate and attend to liturgical needs that may be overlooked in the itinerary of typical worship life. For example, Susan B. Reynolds describes how an occasional service from the Catholic Book of Blessings to bless parents after a stillbirth or miscarriage "made present the gentle hope embodied by Christ who, raised from the dead, returned with his wounds to the site of his hasty burial to wipe the tear-stained cheeks of his dear friends, woman bewildered by grief."[1] Occasional services provide opportunities to show just how deep and wide the liturgical sensibility of an assembly is.

They bring focus upon particular pastoral needs within an assembly. Returning to the stillbirth example, it might help you to know that there is an official United States national recognition of pregnancy loss and stillbirth on October 15—National Pregnancy and Infant Loss Remembrance Day.[2] The day suggests that it is not only mothers who bear the pain of losing an unborn child. Families are devastated as well. How might an occasional service build upon the observations of Bigelow to craft liturgical responses for grieving partners, grandparents, siblings, and other relatives? Occasional services bring awareness to the variety of worship services that may not be generally familiar across traditions. Take, for example, a Seven Last Words service, which is a Good Friday service where homilies are preached based on the seven last sayings of Jesus found across the New Testaments Gospels. They also reserve space for liturgical ingenuity and extraordinary hospitality to host invited guests such as visiting preachers, choirs, musicians, and other artists; leaders of other religious traditions; teachers; elected officials; community leaders and saintly citizens; youth and children; those wise in years; and those whose absence would make any service of Christian worship incomplete.

Imagining Occasional Services

Services of Blessing for School Teachers and Students: This service marks either the beginning or end of the school year (or can occur for both), acknowledging the joys and hardships faced in the classroom and learning process. This service can bring awareness of the learning process to the church community, encourage teachers and students with communal hope and joy, and prompt engagement beyond the sanctuary walls and in the school systems and classrooms.

Celebrations of the Arts: These services are full services dedicated to worshipping God through the arts. It brings together music, dance, visual arts, spoken word and poetry, and creative space design. The artistic representation serves as proclamation (and replaces traditional preaching), prayer, and music making. Oftentimes, these services are held outside of standard worship times; however, I would encourage offering these services during high seasons of the church (i.e., turning a traditional Christmas service into a celebration of the season through the arts).

Services of Lament and Solidarity: Given our global social climate, services of lament and solidarity offer spaces of repentance, witness, hope, and recommitment. These services are usually held in response to major tragedies, generally caused by injustices of any kind, and can also be opportunities to acknowledge the inequality and injustice present in your immediate communities.

Services of Rest: In 2016, Tricia Hersey founded The Nap Ministry, a ministry that curates workshops and sacred spaces of rest as resistance. What if your congregation offered a service of rest? This service can be set up to create an environment for peace and rest for your congregation. It would require flexible space, which may mean moving outside of the sanctuary if possible, or reimagining the use of space if you can only use the sanctuary. A service of rest can be creatively designed by a team of worship leaders and congregation members, with the goal of praising God through intentionally slowing down and celebrating God's gift of rest in the midst of a society built to equate busyness as accomplishment.

Worship on the Lawn (or outdoors): Holding worship services outside of the sanctuary is not a novel discovery, but one that happens less frequently these days. Holding a service on or near the church property, but outside of the actual building develops bridges between the church and the community in new and creative ways. This service requires a lot of advance planning and resources, and there are many opportunities to think differently about worship flow, music choices, leadership representation, and more.

Questions and Exercises

1. Sit down with your worship planning team, or on your own if you are a solo pastor, and think through the various occasional services that are at the heart of your community. List these services on a calendar for the entire year. Observe where these services intersect with liturgical seasons of the church year or take precedence. How do they connect to the liturgical calendar?

2. What does the broad view of your congregation's occasional services tell you about the community? What is the history of these services and how they have functioned within the life of the church?

3. How have the occasional services evolved? What has been lost over the years? What has been added recently? Why?

4. Identify the ritual practices that mark each occasional service. Discuss these practices with either members of your worship leadership or key stakeholders within your congregation, or both. How are these occasions marked? Does anything need to change or be updated? Are the practices inclusive of the entire community? What do these services say about God and God's activity in the congregation?

5. If you were to invent an occasional service, what would be the guiding premise or theme? How might you choose a theme based upon a particular pastoral need in the worshipping assembly that you lead? Perhaps you opt for a worship service without a theme and concentrate on silence with or without conscious prayer, like a centering prayer service, or like that which we have not yet seen or experienced.

6. Worship in Action: Move worship outside of the sanctuary for the specific purpose of engaging in protest or social justice marches (i.e., a Black Lives Matters protest in your community, or a gay pride parade, etc.). Imagine starting worship in your sanctuary, or a designated gathering space within the church. Bring the community together in prayer, and then move out into the streets to worshipfully engage in social activism. Let your congregation know in advance, and consider incorporating activities in the church (prayer, singing, holding space and silence for those marching, etc.) for members of the congregation who are not able to join in the march for whatever reason.

SACRED SPACE

In Exodus 3:5, God instructs Moses, "Don't come any closer! Take off your sandals, because you are standing on holy ground." We may have never heard God speak like God did to Moses (or at all, for that matter). But we know what is meant by "holy ground." Maybe holy ground is right inside our doorway at home, where no matter how our day has gone, our partners, roommates, children, relatives, or just peace and quiet greet us with a consistent and steady embrace. Or, if home is too crazy, maybe holy ground is the resonant floor of the church or the buzz of a cafe, the well-worn carpet of our office, the calm we create within a pair of headphones, or the expanse of nature or what is above the ground, like the night sky. Wherever we find holy ground, there we also enter into sacred space.

Sacred space established for public worship feels different from everyday life. It brings a sense of wonder and awe that sets the space apart from the daily rhythms and routines. Sacred space might comprise the architecture, decorum, and furnishings of a sanctuary. Or, sacred space may be filled with what we could never craft or provide, what is solemnized already as it is, not requiring a special blessing, status, or name from us. In either case or in contexts that balance both the human-made and divine *caritas*, sacred space exudes what Heather Elkins in her review of *Worship Space Acoustics*, describes as, "reverberance, responsiveness, spaciousness, intimacy, and clarity" so that we recognize immediately where we are, on holy ground.[1]

Worship space is dynamic and contributes to the meaning of ritual practices and to the shape and content of the religious system.[2] In *To Take Place*, an exploration of ancient Jewish and early Christian understandings of religious space, Jonathan Z. Smith illustrates how early Christians imbued the idea of holiness upon places. This can be seen in attempts in the fourth century to memorialize places important in the life of Jesus including his birthplace and his tomb. The belief for early Christians was that these places, which we linked closely with crucial points in Jesus's life, were permeated with divine power.[3] These acts of memorializing space, or creating sacred space, illustrate that way in which people and societies create their sacred space, "ascribing sacred meaning to spaces and places that previously had no such meanings ascribed to them."[4]

Human production of sacred space also maps a social hierarchy onto the space. The organization of people within the space imputes levels of power in determining who is allowed in different parts of the sacred space. Establishing least sacred spaces as open for everyone who enters the building, but reserving the most sacred spaces (i.e., the pulpit) only for clergy establishes a dynamic that privileges one group of people to hold power over others. The way in which we organize space and individuals in the space creates dynamics that can be either marginalizing or inclusive. In the process of enlivening sacred space where people gather to encounter God's presence in worship, the goal should be to establish and maintain equitable and inclusive dynamics for all worshippers.

In *Church Architecture*, James F. White and Susan J. White provide detailed pastoral considerations regarding the construction and configuration of sacred space.[5] They point out that visibility and audibility often take precedence in the construction and furnishing of sacred space. Yet disability access is of utmost importance. How are people of all physical and mental abilities made not only to feel welcome, but accommodated and embraced in worship space? White and White write, "At stake here is a vital issue of justice, the need for the church to affirm the full human worth of all individuals."[6] It is crucial to organize and craft sacred space so that it symbolically and functionally empowers all of the people of God for worship, especially those for whom customary architectural scale and social norms often overlook or underestimate.

Frequently visited areas such as the bathrooms and the utility rooms where custodial equipment is held are also a part of the holy of holies. Their condition says a lot about how we attend to hospitality fit for a house of prayer and the importance of honoring those who serve the most essential needs of the church.[7] Cleanliness is not next to godliness. Yet finding a way to build in comfort and not simply sterility into restrooms and workrooms exhibits filigreed care for the spiritual, psychological, and physical health of our neighbors. Here again, accessibility as well as upgrades and amenities are crucial.

Energy conservation also speaks about how sacred space participates in the shared responsibility to care for God's created order. Creation Justice Ministries (who formerly operated as the National Council of Churches Eco-Justice Program until 2013) is an ecumenical nonprofit organization dedicated to equipping and mobilizing Christian communities toward eco-justice transformation.[8] They propose ways congregations can contribute to reducing air pollution and carbon emissions, while also reducing the church's operating costs through reduction of energy use. Some of their recommendations include installing programmable thermostats and replacing broken appliances with energy-efficient models. Weatherizing church buildings, lowering the temperature on the water heater, swapping out Styrofoam and plastic for washable and reusable materials, or building with sustainable materials shows a deeper integration of creation care within sacred space.

In addition to the physical building or architecture and ethical practices, the sacred nature of worship space can be communicated through the sound, lighting, decor, and the exterior presentation. As it relates to sound, we encourage worship leaders to think of silence as sacred space. In speaking of what he calls the "region of Great Silence," Howard Thurman describes silence as the space where "the Presence of God is sensed as an all-pervasive aliveness which materializes into concreteness of communion: the reality of prayer."[9] He continues to say, "Here God speaks without words and the self listens without ears. Here at last, glimpses of the meaning of all things and the meaning of one's own life are seen with all their strivings."[10] While Thurman speaks specifically of a deep inner peace and silence one reaches in personal devotion, we want to imagine how this idea can find its way into a worship service. Though silence is often more associated with the inaudible, think instead of silence as creating sacred space at a moment's notice in a service. Calling for silence in a service interrupts distractions with speechlessness that lofts our liturgical intentions into a shared, vulnerable pause where we can more freely approach and venerate the Divine, unencumbered by trying to say what is more naturally ineffable.

Exploring the integration of lighting, decor, furniture, and liturgical vessels is also important when thinking about sacred space. Matters of scale for pulpit, lectern, font, table, altar rails, pews, and seats all lend themselves to establishing what is sacred, and shape the dynamics of the space. Instead of a very large, elaborate pulpit that remains up on a stage, a lightweight podium that affords flexible use in the space can mediate closer connections between worship leaders and the congregation, and shift the power dynamics. Strategic lighting and light-able surfaces can guide people visually through the tone and feeling of what is taking place in worship. Liturgical vessels like the chalice and paten do not need to be shiny or of great value; yet they should be large and substantial enough to accommodate the elements needed to celebrate the Lord's Supper and also to communicate the profundity of all miracles, immanent and transcendent, happening at the Table. Creating alternative spaces that invite sacred engagement from the community like a prayer wall or a bench for quiet time and meditation on the church lawn creates a connection between an individual's personal devotion and their public worship. These types of spaces extend our imagination of sacred space beyond the limitations of a sanctuary.

Exterior space also bears witness to the light of God. What is it saying to the surrounding neighborhood or district? We may do well just to have the grass cut, the hedges trimmed, and the parking lot free of potholes. Yet a manicured landscape or lot is not what we are bringing into consideration. Tagging the building you use with graffiti or hanging banners from it or leaving it worn on the outside only to conceal a magical interior of spiritual wonder might be far more effective for connecting with the surrounding community. Sometimes, historical preservation complicates how a church maintains its exterior. We recommend approaching negotiations regarding historical preservation as an opportunity to extend an invitation to worship and to involve the church or assembly in community beautification in ways that could build more understanding in larger community-minded conversations of what Christians envision as being worth preserving and maintaining.

With the rise in virtual worship, it is necessary to imagine your digital platforms as sacred space. Paying attention to how you invite worship participants into this virtual experience is key. What does the digital environment look and feel like? How do you use sound to set this time apart from everyday digital engagement? Whether you are worshipping via Zoom, Big Marker, Facebook, Instagram, or YouTube, intentional planning and creativity give us new ways to experience and name spaces as sacred, and should be done with the gathered assembly in mind. Whether physically together or online, sacred spaces are the primary centers where people gather for the celebration of the word of God and encounter refuge, healing, and hope.

Questions and Exercises

1. How much time are you and your worship planning team spending on preparing your space for worship? What are the main priorities you consider? How are you empowering the creativity of your worship planning team in this area? How much of your budget is dedicated to creative and innovative use of the worship space?

2. Does your church have a team dedicated to designing sacred space? If not, how might you consider including such a team? Can you recruit volunteers from within your community? Assemble a small team to focus on the space design for worship. Begin with the major liturgical seasons like Advent, Lent, and Easter. Brainstorm the possibilities of the space with this team, and think critically about who will be in worship. This is an opportunity to recruit and empower volunteers from your community to share in the gifts of worship through imagining and designing sacred space according to your liturgical rhythm.

3. Reflect on your worship services over the last year. How many of those services invited you to be creative with the way you set up the space? Where did you find times when your space did not invite the full participation of those gathered? How might you have changed the space to be more inclusive?

4. As a time of meditation and devotion, spend some time alone walking through your church building. Explore all of the grounds, including the outside area, restrooms, offices, hallways, sanctuary, fellowship hall, and so on. Is the space/environment theologically sound? What power dynamics are expressed through the setup of the space? What does the building communicate regarding who is welcome and who is not? How does the space make room for differently abled bodies in the space? What needs to change in order to ensure a more equitable environment?

5. What are other spaces that are deemed sacred for your congregation beyond the sanctuary? How might you engage your members in conversation to learn more about these spaces? As you are in dialogue, imagine ways to connect the importance of these alternative worship spaces into the areas that are normally privileged for communal worship.

The Reverend Dr. Bonner recalls how a Chattanooga church had a big chalkboard that the community wrote on to share a collective Bucket List: "I suppose this was inspired by the movie, *The Bucket List.*" But it was helping people to explore their mortality and embrace the importance of living abundant life. It was a big hit in the neighborhood and engaged the whole community.

Chapter 17

Ecology and Worship

*Leah D. Schade, assistant professor of preaching and worship at
Lexington Theological Seminary*

From the water that welcomes and washes us at baptism, to the grain and grapes that feed us at the Eucharist, to the church pews hewn from trees that support the gathered assembly, to the very ground upon which we stand and the very air that we breathe to sing, preach, and pray—Christian worship cannot exist without God's Creation.[1] Yet, most Christians take for granted the fact that Creation provides for our worship, and that our liturgical practices are rooted in ancient agrarian rituals centered around the elements and rhythms of nature. We ignore ecology and worship *and* the ecology of worship at our peril. One study has shown, for example, that congregants who attend churches where environmental issues are rarely mentioned have lower concern for issues such as climate change.[2] This same study indicated that Christians are among those who are least responsive to environmental threats. In other words, there are ethical implications for ecology and worship. However, there is also a joyous and deeply spiritual aspect of ecology and worship as well. Worship that acknowledges and embraces God's Creation enables a more robust experience of praise, contemplation, communion, and enactment of justice in the world.

The word *worship* is derived from *weorthscipe*—an Old English term from feudalism acknowledging the worthiness or "worth"-shipness of the lord to whom one owed allegiance.[3] Applied to what we do as a gathered assembly, not only do we ascribe ultimate worth to God, but God has declared worth-ship over everything in the cosmos. At the very beginning, God saw all that had been made and declared it *tov*, good (Genesis 1). According to ecological liturgical scholar Benjamin Stewart, this means that "the horizon of concern in Christian worship extends outward to the entire universe."[4] I would add that the concern of Christian worship is also as close as the land upon which your church has been built, including the trees, plants, animals, and ecosystems that support your worshipping community. At the time of this writing, we have already seen, for example, how metal neurotoxins and lead poisoning have ravaged water supplies in Flint, Michigan, and Newark, New Jersey. Notably, ecological transgressions also disproportionately affect communities of color and lower socioeconomic status. A pandemic is also sweeping the world that many scientists see as a zoonosis, or virus, linked to animal transmission and conceivable as linked to human interference and devastation of natural habitats.[5]

Thus, we must help congregations understand that their church is part of an even larger worshipping community in Creation. The Bible is replete with reminders of the inextricable link between Creation and God's people. Adam (literally, "Earthling") was created from the soil and charged with tilling and keeping Earth (Genesis 2). Jewish rituals revolved around seasons of planting, growth, and harvest, the patterns of which form the basis of the Christian liturgical calendar. Jesus used images from nature (trees, flowers, birds, rocks, weather) to illustrate his teachings and interacted directly with many aspects of Creation (rivers, lakes, seas, winds). The wilderness, mountains, and gardens were places where Jesus sought prayerful refuge. And as I've noted elsewhere, "Nature gave witness to the personhood and divinity of Jesus from the time of his birth announced in the heavens, to the darkness that enveloped the land at his crucifixion. Earth took Jesus into itself and gave witness to the resurrection with earthquake, sunrise, and the beauty of a garden."[6]

Further, biblical writers often address Earth not as an object, but as a subject capable of praising God: "Sing to the LORD a new song! Sing to the LORD, all the earth! . . . The trees of the forest too will shout out joyfully" (Psalm 96:1, 12). Speaking of trees, Matthew Sleeth insists that it's time for us to "reforest our faith" by recognizing that trees play a central role in the salvation story of the Bible. By paying attention to trees in scripture and in our world, all will mutually benefit from this renewal of relationship between humans and nature.[7] Conversely, when we destroy Creation through processes like clear-cutting, mountaintop removal, and the pollution of oceans, we deprive God of worship. We also deprive ourselves of the opportunity to worship within the sanctuary of Earth itself.

Why does this matter? Because there are ethical implications for considering (or disregarding) Creation and worship. For example, how can a church baptize when the local water is polluted from industrial waste, or tainted with lead, or poisoned by fracking effluent dumped in the nearby stream? How can we taste the bread of Communion when we know that agribusiness conglomerates have conscripted land and farmers into ecologically harmful practices that deny God's command for sabbath? How can we drink the wine knowing that climate-fueled wildfires have destroyed millions of acres of vineyards?[8] How can we sing to the Lord a new song when our lungs are wheezing with asthma exacerbated by air pollution? All of this is to say that Christian worship must raise a prophetic voice when the very elements that make worship possible are threatened, compromised, or even a danger to the worshippers themselves.

When worshipping Christians pay attention to the land, air, waterways, and the ecological "neighborhoods" in which their community is situated, they may be compelled to respond with justice and create community.[9] Our baptismal vows call us to address the sins of environmental racism, pollution, wasteful consumerism, and ecological destruction. The Table of Communion, which promises abundance, obliges us to address the systemic sin that results in food deserts where people in rural and urban areas have no access to healthy food. And every worship service reminds us that God so loved *the world* that Jesus's birth, life, death, and resurrection are salvific for all of us—including this living Earth.

Questions and Exercises

1. Create connections between worship and ecology through preaching, hymns that invoke Creation, liturgy that centers around different themes of Creation, and simply by bringing aspects of nature into the worship space such as plants, fish, fountains, and rocks.[10] Offer prayers for those whose vocation involves the sea, forests, farming, caring for animals, and horticulture. Plan rituals of blessing around the seasons and patterns of nature specific for your context. Use resources such as the "Season of Creation" for specific ideas.[11]

2. Take a walk around your church building with your fellow worshippers (especially children and youth) and list all the living things you encounter. Whether your church is in an urban, suburban, coastal, or rural setting, learn the scientific names for the insects, flowers, trees, and animals you find. During the liturgical prayers, lift up these fellow worshippers and ask for hearts to be moved to protect the sanctity of God's Creation.

3. Plan an outdoor worship service at a campground, city park, or other natural location. Remind worshippers that when John's Gospel refers to the "Word made flesh" in 1:14, this flesh came from the living substance of this Earth. Jesus was a person who drank this water, walked on this ground. Jesus lived among us on this planet we call home.

4. When celebrating the rituals of baptism and Communion, offer opportunities to live into God's call to justice and righteousness. Frame practices of advocacy for clean water, food justice, nature preserves, and climate action as an embodiment of our Christian vocation.

5. When planning for weddings, encourage couples to consider ways to reign in excessive spending and decrease their carbon footprint when it comes to travel, food purchases for the reception, and the ceremony itself. When offering pastoral care for planning funerals, suggest families consider a "green burial" for a more natural way to dispose of

human remains that avoids the chemicals, concrete, and extravagant coffins, while still maintaining the dignity and beauty of the ritual.

6. Announce during worship public opportunities for climate justice, such as local protests, marches, and rallies. Perhaps mobilize the assembly that you lead in worship to provide prayer or nourishment such as cups of water and snacks to those in grassroots and frontline advocacy for creation care and ecological repair and celebration.

Part Two

DEEPENING THE WORK OF THE PEOPLE

EMBODIMENT IN WORSHIP

What comes to mind when you hear the words *embodiment* and *worship* together? Dance? Walking? Bodies in motion? Do you cringe at the idea of even thinking about bodies in worship? Or do you leap with joy and imagine all the ways bodies move about the worship space? There are a variety of reactions invoked by the idea of embodiment in worship, and any of these reactions offers insight into an individual's personal experiences of bodies in worship. While people might first think about and define embodiment in worship as movement (i.e., dance or procession), I want us to draw an understanding of embodiment in worship as a *total awareness of our bodies in the space and time of worship*. The total awareness I am describing encompasses a 360-degree consciousness of how we experience and engage (or disengage) in worship at any given point of a worship service, in relationship to our own bodies and the bodies of others worshipping with us. Thinking about the different ways our bodies react to particular points of the worship service creates opportunities for deeper thought in worship planning to ensure that we are sensitive to engaging the gathered community in a multiplicity of ways. People enter into worship with a particular way of knowing their own bodies, and the way we know our own bodies shapes the way we know and experience God in worship.

In her book *The Worshiping Body*, Kimberly Bracken Long claims our bodies are central to all of our experiences. She states, "To consider worship as an embodied event is to explore all the various ways bodies are involved in meeting God."[1] If this is the case, then we can assume that our bodies carry memory, and all that we carry in our bodies enters into worship with us and shapes the way we engage worship of God and our worship practice. Everything we hear and do in worship evokes a bodily response. Therefore, embodiment is all about being aware and sensitive to our bodies' involvement in worship.

This heightened awareness of the body's involvement in worship is especially important for worship planning and leadership. A focus on the body helps worship leaders establish any environment of worship as a site in which we are able to bring our whole selves to the worship moment—mind, body, and spirit. Long believes this integration of our whole selves into worship mirrors the realities of personal faith development, in which body and mind work in concert to nurture faith.[2] Connecting the lived experience of our faith journey with our public worship invites a deeper sense of connection to the worship practice and to the worshipping community. When the fullness of who we are is welcomed into worship and invited to connect to the fullness of those around us with special attention to embodiment, we create opportunities to see God differently in the moment of liturgical practice. Worship leaders can simply raise awareness of the different bodies around us in the space. Or they can invite a new way of allowing one's body to be present. For example, an invitation to stillness and silence might liturgically reorient in a very different way someone who is used to a very high-energy and loud worship experience.

As a dancer, I, Khalia, know and experience God in and through my own body, and this is a result of being deeply aware of my own body through my dance training. Therefore, it may be easier for someone with experiences that are rooted in their body to feel God's presence in worship through expressed movements or rhythms of music. This is just one example of how our knowledge of our own bodies shapes our knowledge and engagement with God. In worship planning, it is important to acknowledge that we all gather with different levels of awareness of our bodies. Based upon this shared realization, we can then begin to create opportunities for that awareness to be stretched as we desire for our knowledge of God to be stretched. We can alter worship in very simple ways, or in grand gestures, depending on the congregational capacity for embracing an embodied focus in worship.

Finally, realizing the centrality of the body in worship practice and the worshipping community liberates a congregation to recognize all of the bodies in the space, including bodies that are marginalized. This is especially true for differently abled bodies. When we are aware of bodies in worship and shift our focus in worship toward the integration of the whole self, we are then able to connect more deeply to the entire community and begin to privilege the bodies that are often ignored or overlooked in the space. This shift of focus and liturgical power helps us to think critically about what we say (*are we acknowledging those who may not be able to stand when we invite the congregation to stand and sing?*), or about who is present and where in the space (*are all of the leadership male bodies?*), or who we think holds power (*do children have an opportunity to be in spaces of liturgical authority?*). Opening up our communities to expand, and even transform, the places of liturgical authority through embodiment in worship allows the congregation to truly see and value all persons gathered to worship, and invites the possibilities of new and imaginative ritual practices that are shaped from the bodies, minds, and spirits of the congregation. This process can produce beautiful and new ways of engaging God and community in worship.

Sometimes there can be tension in moving bodies to the central focus of our worship, in planning, in leadership, and in execution. Because our bodies are different, and we connect to God in worship in different ways, and because society views different bodies in particular ways, there can be apprehension or timidity in engaging a focus on embodiment. In these cases, the pastor and worship leaders must be creative in this engagement, without being overbearing or too instructive. Sometimes you will have to model embodiment in small ways (gestures, language, etc.) that are hospitable and not intimidating, and we must do this work remembering *the body is the locus of the experience of the holy*.[3]

Questions and Exercises

1. Recall a service you attended that encouraged you to pay greater attention to your body. What happened in the service that made you heighten your focus on your body in worship? What words were spoken? How did the space contribute to the experience? What

do you remember about the people who were in worship with you? What lessons do you take from this service to help you think about embodiment in worship?

2. Recall a service you've experienced where embodiment was not incorporated in worship. How did the service feel? How did you feel in the service? What do you remember of the people in worship with you? What words were spoken? What were the actions and movement of the gathered community? How could these actions and movements been used to demonstrate embodiment? What lessons do you take from this service to help you think about embodiment in worship?

3. What are services or ritual practices within your community that are inherently embodied? (E.g., baptism, anointing services, right hand of fellowship, etc.) How can these practices be used to encourage a greater awareness of embodiment within your congregation? How are these services taking into consideration the different bodies in the worship space? In what ways can bodies that are often marginalized be centered in these ritual practices?

4. Becoming more aware of the body in worship takes practice, and it is great to do the work with others. In a small group, read the following scriptures aloud and take five minutes for each scripture to think about and discuss your responses to the questions below.

    I. Scriptures to Read:

        a. Psalm 23

        b. Psalm 47

        c. Psalm 136

    II. Discussion Questions for the Scriptures

        a. How did your body respond to hearing each scripture?

        b. Where were your resistance points? Your comfort points?

c. What resistance and comfort can you imagine others having to tone and language and message of the scriptures?

d. What strategies might you use in worship planning with these scriptures to encourage a congregational awareness of embodied responses?

e. What bodily engagement (i.e., movement) do you imagine with each scripture? (Feel free to try this exercise with the scriptures being used in your upcoming worship services.)

Connecting the Congregation

How do you get a congregation on board with this idea of embodiment in worship? Start by introducing it through the language and gestures used in worship leadership. Being a model of awareness of the body is an important first step. For example, if you are introducing a moment of prayer, think about how you might invite the congregation to engage their bodies in prayer. Simple words like *posture* or *bring your whole selves to pray* or *remain silent as you become aware of how God is speaking to you and in you* are very helpful ways of increasing mindfulness. Take small steps of progress, be true to who is in your congregation, and leverage those who have high bodily awareness in your leadership.

ENCLAVE WORSHIP AND CHRIST'S CALL FOR UNITY

Christian worship is never neutral. It always takes on the characteristics of the environment in which it happens and the people who practice it. In a sense, therefore, worshippers in any given context of worship constitute an enclave, or a gathering of particular people in a particular place set apart for a particular social, cultural, and political purpose. Here, enclave worship generically describes the worship practices of communities united by particular markers of human identity in God. Enclave worship is crucial for expressing the fullness of Christ's body. Yet we also want to raise God's apocalyptic vision of unity and look to it as a *telos*—or earth-as-it-is-in-heaven aim—that ought to be a core commitment for any worshipping community.

There are reasons to worship in an enclave. A Taiwanese Presbyterian church may want to preserve specific cultural identifiers such as language or a disposition toward family or work. A Native American congregation may deeply interweave indigenous ancestral customs in order to distinguish their faithfulness to Christianity from the Christians who virtually eliminated all conditions for them to live as a free tribe. A Puerto Rican Pentecostal assembly may want to distinguish themselves from Mexican and Dominican siblings in Christ. Yet even in those liturgical acts of community orientation, it is crucial to understand that a commitment to shared cultural preservation does not suggest uniformity. Nor does it preclude liturgical diversity.

Wide-ranging diversity exists within a congregation and communities sharing essentialized political identities that may appear ethnically homogenous. Facility with the Taiwanese language may differ between the first and subsequent generations who embody the church. Cherokee churches are not uncommon. Yet a Lenape-led community of faith such as the Ujima Village Christian Church of Pennington, New Jersey, continues to defy the odds.[1] Political viewpoints may also veer from one another within the same family and certainly within a congregation.

The "Black church" is likewise not monolithic. A Coptic American congregation's celebration of the Nativity will happen a week after Afro-Caribbean Pentecostal Christmas and watch night services. Other African American churches will celebrate Kwanzaa in the transition from Christmastide to the new year. An African American congregation deeply committed to its African heritage may choose to privilege African spirituality such as Ghanaian *sankofa*—returning the wisdom of the past in order to move into the future knowledgeably—within their Christian expression as a way of resisting and subverting the Christianity that enslaved their ancestors and was used as a violent tool of power. Or they might electrify their commitments to abolishing white supremacy and anti-Black racism in Juneteenth celebrations that involve ecclesial protest as well as liturgical revelry. Afro-Catholic Mass might begin with a procession of dance and percussion while African American Episcopalian communities may choose to infuse spirituals into evensong. Still another Black congregation may focus as much upon queer equality as it does upon matters of racial justice. Matters of identity, heritage, geographic regions, doctrinal commitments, and socioeconomic status all impact enclave communities' ways of being, which deepens the shared and common connection within each individual community in worship, while also lending a great deal of diversity.[2]

In the chapters that follow, we have invited guest contributors to think about how practices of worship perhaps associated with enclave communities have distinct theological know-how and *phronesis*, or practical wisdom, for any community of worship. While the following discussion of diversity in worship is in no way comprehensive, it is our hope and prayer that the sample of worship considerations with respect to human diversity will help worship leaders within any context live into the vision of God to unite all people in praise and thanksgiving before the Lamb (Revelation 7:9).

Questions and Exercises

1. While enclave worship has its merits and critical importance with respect to celebrating diversity within the body of Christ, if we take the creation narratives of Genesis seriously, that we share the same parentage from God and are flesh of one another's flesh, believe in the ministry of Jesus of Nazareth evolving to welcome the Gentiles, hold on to the power of the miracle of many tongues provided by the Holy Spirit at Pentecost, and look forward to the future of Revelation where every tribe, nation, and people praise the Lamb, how much of our worship leadership should be dedicated to welcoming any and all into the forgiveness and everlasting love of God?

2. How can you imagine enclave communities responding to and advancing the call to unity in the body of Christ through their particularity? Thinking about immigrant communities, how might spaces of enclave worship be integral in the incorporation of the community members into larger society (general, denominational, communal), while also being a place of refuge?

3. Enclave worship communities have unique organizational structures including family-style gatherings, worship that features very little lay participation, smaller community-style gatherings focused on building community with the larger membership, or a structure that takes on more interest in the civic and political affairs of the surrounding community. Assess what enclave communities you find within your own congregation. Remember, oftentimes we have enclaves present within the larger community as well. What does the structure(s) you find say about the needs of the members within the community? How does it inform you about your worship and connection with the congregation?

Chapter 20
WORSHIP AND DISABILITY

Rebecca F. Spurrier, associate dean for worship life and assistant professor of worship at Columbia Theological Seminary

Christian worship requires an assembly of people who worship God together. Yet not every worshipper has the same access to the spaces, times, and forms of prayer and praise that constitute public worship. Embedded in every liturgical element—prayers, songs, sermons, Communion, practices of gathering and sending—are assumptions about the bodies and abilities of each person who has gathered. These assumptions often do not take into account the full spectrum of what it means to be human nor all of the ways that those who worship experience and encounter God. Instead they assume and privilege particular kinds of bodies and abilities.[1]

Disability Studies is an academic discipline that questions how we come to understand what it means to be "normal" and how societies enforce particular expectations for "normalcy."[2] Disability Studies privileges and prioritizes human differences over human sameness or similarities, challenging the idea that there is a normal human body. Every person moves through and navigates the world differently, but social, cultural, and political worlds are designed to accommodate, support, and sustain some bodies more than others. Disability Studies critiques a medical model of disability that interprets disability as a matter of individual responsibility and as a tragic or pitiable condition to be prevented, healed, or overcome. Rather it focuses attention on the social and political structures that need to be transformed to support disabled lives as well as on the knowledge, wisdom, and experience of disabled people and communities. In a world in which disability is a common experience, human societies need the wisdom and witness of disabled communities to navigate human embodiment and "imagined futures."[3]

To begin with human differences and to center disability experience in worship challenges beliefs about human ability that have profoundly shaped Christian theology and worship. In *The Disabled God*, theologian Nancy Eiesland identifies some important ways that Christian churches have failed or harmed people with disabilities. These failures occur through inadequate theologies of disability. First, in the concept of sin-disability conflation, disability is associated directly or indirectly with sin in the world.[4] In some Christian communities it is assumed that a person is born with or experiences a disability because of a particular sin that she or he or that person's family has committed. Other Christians assume that disability exists because the world is sinful, evil, or fallen. In the future that God promises, when evil and sin are no longer present, there will no longer be any disability or disabled people; the church pursues a vision of the world without disabilities. In yet another example, Christians imagine sin in human life by using disability metaphorically, evoking blindness, deafness, or other disabilities to name human wrongdoing, failure, or complicity. Thus, in both implicit and explicit ways disability becomes associated with sin, evil, or tragedy.

Second, in the practice of identifying disability with "virtuous suffering," disabled people are encouraged to understand their disabilities and the unjust social barriers they encounter as a form of "divine testing."[5] Prayers for the healing of disabilities frequently evoke the power of God in ways that approach disability as inspiration for abled Christians. Disabled people are viewed as those with special needs or gifts rather than as ordinary Christians or what Eiesland calls "historical actors and theological subjects."[6]

Third, in the practice of segregationist charity, churches seek to help people with disabilities or create special programs for them but do not want to change theologies, symbols, or practices regarding disability and access in order to acknowledge and affirm the role that people with disabilities have within the life and work of the church.[7] Such communities prefer not to address the harmful understandings of disability that pervade sermons, hymns, and prayers nor the aesthetics and preferences that bolster ableism in worship. Again disabled people are perceived as in need of the church's help rather than as Christian subjects who have contributions to make to Christian worship.

To identify harmful theologies of disability and to imagine spaces where all of us who gather for worship have access to God and to one another is vital work for the people of God. This work will involve conversion to new ways of naming and transforming ableism in worship and beyond. Planning worship with the assumption of one kind of body-mind is easier and more familiar than to anticipate that God has created and loves many different ways of being an embodied creature in the world. Yet if worship is "humanity at full stretch," our common prayer requires that we bring all of what it means to be human to God. For in worship we offer to God the fullness of the humanity that God has both created and saved, the fullness of the humanity that God entered into through the incarnation of Jesus Christ.[8] We also rehearse a vision of the beloved community where worshipping God is a foretaste of the kind of spaces where all creatures of God flourish together with and before God. In order to rehearse this vision Christians must actively name and address the barriers that prevent disabled Christians from participation in worship and from leadership in the church.

Questions and Exercises

1. "Nothing about Us without Us" was a rallying call of the disability rights movement.[9] As churches transform their practices and relationships with disability, it is imperative to center the perspectives and experiences of disabled people both within and outside. Actively and intentionally invite disabled worshippers to offer their gifts and expertise in worship planning and leadership. Encourage and develop structures for all worshippers to provide feedback on barriers that they experience in worship as well as ways that they

would like to be included in worship. When disabled people identify inclusive worship practices, believe their experiences and respond accordingly.

2. Disabled people should not be expected to teach abled people about ableism in worship and in the world. Those of us who are abled have a responsibility to educate ourselves and to nurture theological imagination informed by experiences of disability. Identify and support educational forums and other learning opportunities that engage theologies and histories of disability. For example, a small group might discuss Nancy Eiesland's *The Disabled God* or the documentary *Crip Camp*. Such forums will invite congregants to confess harms the church has done to people with disabilities and seek conversion to new ways of understanding disability and embodiment.

3. Those of us who plan worship assume particular kinds of human bodies and abilities. Develop regular practices of interrogating these assumptions: what are people expected to be able to do to participate in communal worship of God and why? Seek common practices for worship that are accessible to more people. At the same time, encourage multiple forms of participation rather than make one practice normative and some people's participation an exception to the norm. Make provisions for multi-modal practices in ways that are not tokenistic so that all forms of participation are supported and encouraged and so that Christian unity is not conflated with uniformity in worship. Learn from disability communities about best practices for access.

4. Participation of people with and without disabilities in worship requires attention to access across many different church spaces. Use resources that have been developed by or in consultation with disabled people to perform an accessibility audit of congregational spaces, times, and practices, from parking lots to pulpits, from baptismal pools to bathrooms, from visual presentations to online worship spaces. Work diligently to identify short- and long-term solutions to barriers.

5. Many congregations respond to people with disabilities by cultivating a posture of charity toward "them" rather than an understanding of people with disabilities as those of us with gifts for ministry and leadership in congregations. Actively support paths to

leadership for congregants with disabilities. Identify structural and theological barriers that prevent disabled people from serving as pastors and worship leaders in the church and work alongside disabled Christians who seek to remove these barriers.

6. Rehearsing a vision of the flourishing of all people in public worship is intimately related to the ways that lives are valued or devalued in other spaces and times throughout the week. Engage the work of disability activists and disability-led organizations to learn about issues from housing and health care to employment and transportation that affect the presence and absence of disabled worshippers in church. Such relationships will change the ways churches pray for, preach about, and partner with disabled people and communities and rehearse the kin-dom of God.

Worship, Gender, and Sexuality

Stephanie A. Budwey, Luce Dean's Faculty Fellow Assistant Professor of the history and practice of Christian worship and the arts, Vanderbilt Divinity School

In considering the interrelationship between worship, gender, and sexuality, it is helpful to begin with Teresa Berger's statement that "the foundational materiality in Christian worship is the bodily presence of worshippers."[1] First and foremost, humans cannot worship without their bodies. Berger goes on to write that "worship is an embodied practice and therefore never gender-free."[2] Because worship is an embodied practice, when humans come to worship, they come with their bodies, including their particular genders and sexualities,[3] as well as differences of race, class, ethnicity, and ability, all of which are inscribed—whether consciously or unconsciously—in worship.

What is deemed "acceptable" regarding gender and sexuality in one worshipping context may not be acceptable in another. Human beings worship "within specific cultural contexts and their particular gender systems, codes, and hierarchies,"[4] and so critical eyes must be brought to worship practices in considering who is included or excluded and who is given power or made invisible because of either their gender or sexuality, or both. As Marjorie Procter-Smith writes, is "the liturgy the work of the people when so many of the people are rendered invisible and silent"?[5] In order to understand why some people are rendered invisible and silent in worship because of either their gender or sexuality, or both, it is helpful to consider Christianity's views on the body.

The Christian church has a "complex, constantly shifting relationship with the body which goes right back into the tips of Christianity."[6] Despite being "an incarnational religion that claims to set captives free, . . . it underpins many of the restrictive practices that body politics expose. In some cases Christianity has been the instigator of these practices because of its dualistic vision of the world."[7] Christianity, drawing from Greek philosophy, has wrestled with the dualism of body and soul from Paul's discussion of the flesh and spirit, to Augustine's struggles with bodily desires, to the Reformation's move away from the materiality of Roman Catholicism, which was further emphasized by the Enlightenment and Descartes's emphasis on the mind and reason over the body.[8] Liturgically this has played out in "anxieties surrounding bodily flows," in questions about priestly celibacy, whether or not people can either attend worship or receive Communion, or both, after sexual intercourse, and whether women can attend worship during menstruation and after giving birth.[9]

In addition to the tensions between the body and the soul, Christianity has also grappled with gender differences. Adrian Thatcher explains how Christianity has adopted the one-sex and two-sex models as outlined in Thomas Laqueur's *Making Sex: Body and Gender from the Greeks to Freud* (1990) and why it is important to understand Scripture and tradition in light of these two models that so profoundly shaped them.[10] With the one-sex model, there is only one sex, "man," and women are seen as "inferior versions of men" or "failed males."[11] According to Laqueur's theory, this was the predominant model until the eighteenth century when the two-sex model replaced it, which posited that there are "two distinct and 'opposite' sexes," female and male.[12] In both of these models, women are seen as inferior to men, leading to liturgical practices of women and men being spatially separated in worship, ritual ordering by gender, and women's exclusion from liturgical leadership, including ordination.[13] Some churches have taught and continue to teach that these hierarchies of gender and sexuality are "natural" and "God-given."

As Berger describes, the twentieth- and twenty-first centuries have witnessed great cultural shifts resulting in "the crumbling of traditional gender codes" and "new and diverse ways of doing gender."[14] Liturgically, this has resulted in some churches ordaining women and LGBTQIA+ individuals.[15] This includes historic moments such as the Reverend Dr. Cameron Partridge becoming the first openly transgender priest to preach at the Washington National Cathedral in Washington, DC in 2014[16] and the Reverend Kori Pacyniak becoming the first transgender, nonbinary priest in the Roman Catholic Womanpriests movement in 2020.[17] Additionally, churches have seen the development of new liturgies such as the blessing and marriage of same-sex couples as well as services of renaming for transgender folx.[18] Despite these positive advances, many instances of liturgical exclusion based on gender and sexuality continue to happen.

According to Jaci Maraschin, "Sexual exclusion originates from the narrowing of our bodily (and sexual) possibilities" and it is "the worst of all exclusions because it denies God's creation, at the centre of which is the human heart."[19] Worshipping communities should be an embodied realization of the eschatological vision where all human beings are treated equally as they are included at and welcomed to God's Table at the Great Banquet (Luke 14), a place where all are able to maintain the particularities of their genders and sexualities they have defined for themselves, and where the hierarchies and oppressions we as humans have attached to these differences disappear.

Thatcher argues that many Christian doctrines—which are expressed throughout the liturgy in prayers, creeds, and congregational songs—such as "the assumed masculinity of the Father of God, the importance attached to the maleness of the incarnate Christ and of the Twelve, [and] the lesser imaging of God by women" are "better understood" when seen through the lens of the one-sex theory, rendering them "more easily transformable."[20] Keeping this approach in mind, how might certain aspects of the liturgy be reenvisioned to be more inclusive of multiple genders and sexualities?

Liturgical language is formative. It shapes understandings of who we are, who God is, and how we relate to one another.[21] Christianity teaches that all humans are made in the image of God, and therefore "it is also important to have multiple images of God"[22] to represent the "multiplicity of human embodiment."[23] Sallie McFague argues for the use of numerous images of God, saying that "*many* metaphors and models are necessary, that a piling up of images is essential, both to avoid idolatry and to attempt to express the richness and variety of the divine-human relationship."[24]

Nicola Slee further describes the need for "a multiplicity of embodied, erotic and queer images of God (and particularly Christ), as necessary to the complex work of personal and political integration with which prayer is charged."[25]

While feminist theologians fought to change liturgical language to include women (e.g., brothers *and* sisters, calling God "Mother," and using "humankind" rather than "mankind"), these changes often retain a binary understanding of gender, excluding all those who identify as nonbinary.[26] It is therefore important to use expansive and inclusive language. Expansive language is language about/for God that "seeks to tell us as much truth about God as we can, utilizing the full range of language available to us. It does not displace traditional language for God, but uses additional metaphors."[27] Inclusive language is language about/for humanity that recognizes that "our language often has built-in biases that exclude and harm some persons. When exclusive language is used, we fall short of our calling to respect all who are created in the image of God."[28]

The need for expansive and inclusive language includes not only spoken prayers but also congregational song.[29] One collection that seeks to do so while also highlighting the work of LGBTQIA+ composers is The Hymn Society of the United States and Canada's *Songs for the Holy Other: Hymns Affirming the LGBTQIA2S+ Community* (2019).[30] There is also scholarship on how music reinforces gender norms (masculine cadences = strong, feminine cadences = weak) and how these normative ideals may be disrupted.[31] Alisha Lola Jones's work explores how "the binary gender framework that the American public expects" (women sing high and men sing low) is challenged by countertenors—"men who sing high"—in worship.[32]

Finally, it is important to pay attention to artwork in liturgical spaces, which can consciously and subconsciously reinscribe normative ideals about gender and sexuality. Sarah Coakley notes that although many claim that God is "beyond gender," most representations of God are gendered, "often in forms which vividly display cultural assumptions about 'normative' gender roles."[33] It is therefore imperative to offer diverse images of the Trinity that can disrupt normative assumptions, including Edwina Sandys's "Christa" (1975), an image of a female Christ,[34] or David Hayward's image of a queer Black Jesus called "Neither" (2014).[35] May these and all aspects of worship celebrate the diversity that is human gender and sexuality.

Questions and Exercises

1. In thinking about liturgical language (prayers and congregational songs), what names and pronouns for God, Jesus, and the Holy Spirit (expansive language) are used in your worship context? Are they masculine, feminine, or nonbinary? Is there a balance of each, or is one name or pronoun used more than others?

2. What language is used to describe human beings (inclusive language)? Are they masculine, feminine, or nonbinary? Are there people who might be made to feel either invisible, excluded, or inhuman, or all of these, by this language?

3. What images for God, Jesus, and the Holy Spirt are found in your worship space? Are they masculine, feminine, or nonbinary? What gender or sexuality norms do they reinforce?

4. What language or images for God, Jesus, and the Holy Spirit resonate with you? What stretches and challenges your imagination?

5. In your worship context, which bodies are either excluded, policed, or both, either by their inability to inhabit certain liturgical spaces, to fully participate in worship, or to assume liturgical leadership (lay and ordained)? What gender and sexuality codes are being reinforced by excluding these bodies?

Chapter 22

LATINX WISDOM FOR WHOLISTIC WORSHIP

Lis Valle-Ruiz, assistant professor of homiletics and worship, and director
of community worship life at McCormick Theological Seminary

Fiesta, with singing and dancing, is the shortest way to describe the multiple expressions of Hispanic and Latinx Christian worship in the United States of America (hereinafter, USA). Take for example the collection of essays, *¡Alabadle! Hispanic Christian Worship*. According to historian, theologian, and editor of the collection, Justo González, the common thread running through all the essays, written by eight different Latinx scholars, is the celebrative character of worship. González explains that "Latino worship is a fiesta . . . a celebration of the mighty deeds of God."[1] Latinx worship is emotional, festive, a family celebration, characterized by movement and sensuality, interactive, a fiesta of the people of God.[2] Pedrito U. Maynard-Reid, professor of biblical studies and missiology, also refers to Hispanic worship as a fiesta of celebration and liberation.[3] One of the main ways in which Latinx worship celebrates divine liberation is *coritos*.[4]

Coritos are short repetitive communal songs, which are, according to Maynard-Reid, "without question the most popular contemporary type of congregational song among Hispanics."[5] The authors of *Latina Evangélicas* define the word *corito* as "a short musical refrain, usually based on a biblical text, either of praise or lament."[6] Through *coritos*, Latinx worshipping communities also recite and interpret scripture. Furthermore, *coritos* might also reveal confessions and theological reflection.

Coritos might not be intended to be confessions or theological treatises, but through *coritos*, the people of God express theological stances. As Zaida Maldonado-Pérez states, "Coritos are normally not expositions about God; they are not theological treatises put to music. Rather, they are very personal, colloquial reflections of a relational theology based on Scripture's reference to us as familia—'sons and daughters of God,' heirs of all the privileges that come to those who are de la casa."[7] They might be colloquial, or even shallow, but they are theological reflections nonetheless.[8]

As reflective of theology, *coritos* might be regarded as sung creeds. Such is the perception of Jonathan García, Pentecostal missionary and MDiv student at McCormick Theological Seminary. In a worship course, García expressed his disagreement with Pentecostal theologian Samuel Soliván's conclusion that Pentecostals are noncreedal. For García, while it may be true that Pentecostals do not have written creeds or confessions, they do have sung creeds in the form of *coritos*.[9] Whether you agree with Solivàn or García, the fact remains that the authors of *Latina Evangélicas* used the lyrics of *coritos* as evidence of what Evangélicas and Protestants believe about salvation, the Trinity, the Spirit, and God's real presence in the midst of the worshipping assembly. Similarly, the Reverend Carmelo Álvarez, author of *El ministerio de la adoración cristiana*, has espoused Pentecostal eschatology, pneumatology, and theological reflection on discipleship through the analysis of *coritos*.[10] The attention that scholars pay to the theological stances that *coritos* profess confirms Martell-Otero's conclusion that coritos are, among others, authoritative texts for Latinx worshippers.[11]

Coritos are not limited to the cognitive, though. *Coritos nos alegran la fiesta en voz y movimiento corporal.* Through short worship songs, Latinx persons at worship enliven the party as they proclaim the mighty deeds of God today and profess their scripture interpretation and creeds, not only in rhythmic work but also in body movement. Movement and physicality are characteristic in Hispanic worship. "Hispanic worship is vocal, physical and interactive" is how Maynard-Reid describes it.[12] Greetings are physical. People embrace as they come into the sanctuary, during the passing of the peace, and before they leave.[13] During *coritos*, "In many churches, both Catholic and Protestant, worshippers move and/or clap to the rhythm as they sing. They seem to dance to the tunes of the coritos and at times they are actually dancing."[14] Worshippers in the Caribbean and Mesoamérica have been singing and dancing their sacred stories for over six hundred years.[15] The rhythms and the words may change as time goes by, but Latinx Wisdom for Worship is holistic as worshippers bring their whole self in the practice of *coritos*. Maynard-Reid describes holistic worship as involving the whole person, including cognition and body, not limited to the intellectual, but rather integrating mind, body, and spirit.[16] Words, music, rhythm, bodies in movement, scripture stories, and theological stances all come together in the singing and dancing of *coritos*.

Questions and Exercises

1. Think about your favorite praise or lament song. Examine the lyrics. What theological stances are you professing when you sing it? What scripture passages does the song quote or reference, if any? What is the interpretation of such scripture passages that the song offers? Is that interpretation true to your own or to that of your faith tradition? If so, how? If not, what changes would you have to make so that it becomes a sung creed true to you or to your faith tradition?

2. Think about your favorite praise or lament song. Examine the music, rhythm, and instruments that generate its sonic phenomenon. What culture(s) does the song reflect and keep alive through music? Do you belong to that culture? Do you listen to the same kinds of music in or out of worship or sacred circles? Why yes or why not? Examine your own level of comfort with moving or dancing while singing. Do you dance when you sing your favorite songs that are not considered sacred or worship music? Do you

dance when you sing sacred or worship music? Do you do it as part of corporate worship or alone at home? Why?

3. Visit a Hispanic/Latinx church other than your own and observe the ways in which people move. Compare and contrast with how people move in your own faith or worshipping community. What is similar? What is different? What would need to happen in worship for both communities to worship together and feel at home? Use your own embodied experience at both places, along with your observations and conversations with other parishioners to generate a proposal related to music and body movement.

4. Write and choreograph a *corito*. What is your favorite scripture verse or biblical story? What does that story do for you (inspire, teach, comfort, etc.)? What do you think the verse or story means? Put those elements together in a short song that you can sing repeatedly. Add music and move to its rhythm in ways authentic to you and your cultural heritage(s).

WORSHIP AND WHITENESS

*Andrew Wymer, assistant professor of liturgical studies at
Garrett-Evangelical Theological Seminary*

Christians worship within the context of racialization. Brian Bantum writes, "The modern world is a racial world. It is a world whose economies are driven by the processes of identification and differentiation . . ." in which, "Christians are not only victims but also perpetrators, killers, and killed alike."[1] Hierarchies of race profoundly shape Christian worship. Race and colonial systems of white power shape how individual worshippers, worshipping communities, and liturgical traditions encounter God through liturgical practices, and the accrual of the centuries-long impact of racialization and its interwoven inequities can be traced through centuries of liturgical history to our present-day practices.

Identifying the role of worship in the emergence of contemporary notions of race in European colonies in North America in the seventeenth century is crucial to understanding worship and race today. In her work *The Baptism of Early Virginia*, historian Rebecca Goetz recounts how Christian rituals, particularly baptism and marriage, were central to the formation and imposition of racial hierarchies in seventeenth-century colonial Virginia.[2] During this time, the theories and practices of worship rituals were adapted by European colonists to validate and enforce a racial order in which "white" Europeans consolidated power to economically exploit persons deemed not white. This is crucial to any examination of race and worship, because it reveals that the practices and theories of Christian worship have always been susceptible to the violent racialized agenda of whiteness.

However, this is only part of the story of the still-unfolding racialized drama of Christian worship. Christian worship has helped those deemed not white and targeted by systems of racialized violence to survive. As Cláudio Carvalhaes writes, "While empires and colonization processes tried to fix rituals as a way of controlling senses, understandings, and bodies, colonized people have always intervened in these processes, creating, rebelling, challenging, undoing, and redoing."[3] For those not deemed white, Christian worship has over the past centuries frequently been a significant site of the contestation and disruption of racial hierarchies and racialized violence and a source of strength to resist the brutality of racialized violence.[4]

95

In our age of "color-blind" racism in which many persons claim that they "do not see color" even while racialized violence and racist inequity are rampant, it is crucial to identify the past and present impact of race on our persons, communities, and, for the sake of this exercise, our worship.[5] Critically reading liturgical history through the lens of race can widen our awareness of both the broader systemic economic, political, and social violence of whiteness and the racialized violence that too frequently occurs in worship itself. Racialized liturgical violence can take any number of forms that may include but not be limited to: (1) forced or coerced ritual participation; (2) widespread building and maintenance of Christian worship sites on stolen land utilizing the economic plunder of racialized violence; (3) enforced subordination or segregation of racially minoritized worshippers and worshipping communities; (4) racially dominant appropriation of liturgical resources created by racially minoritized persons and communities; (5) centering of white practices and theologies as normative; (6) subjugation of racially minoritized bodies, worship experiences, practices, and theories; (7) brutal terrorism of racially minoritized worshipping bodies and sites of worship; and (8) widespread disregard for and silence about the sustained brutal realities of racial violence.

The complex and ongoing legacy of Christian worship within the context of racism and ongoing lynching of Black persons, state and state-sponsored corporate violence against indigenous persons, brutal imprisonment of nonwhite refugees and immigrants in state-run concentration camps, and other expressions of racialized violence necessitate an urgent reckoning with the past and present role of Christian worship in creating and enforcing racial hierarchies and inequities. Such a reckoning requires us to intentionally recognize the impact of race on Christian worship and to critically engage that with attention to broader systems of white domination in the US. This requires leaders and practitioners of Christian worship to carefully explore the impact of racialization on those who worship, on the practices of worship through which we engage our racialized bodies and the racialized bodies of others, and on the theories undergirding our worship that may either reinforce or subvert racialized biases and hegemony. We must account for the racial dominance embedded in the theories and practices of our liturgical traditions as we work to craft a more racially just trajectory for our liturgical traditions and the world. This may require from some of us an intense deconstruction of our personal, communal, and liturgical formation amid the context of systemic and internalized racism.

Questions and Exercises

1. Consider the impact of racialization on the land upon which you worship. Visit a library and research the history of the land, your community, and how it came to be occupied by non-native persons and a site of Christian worship. Ask, "Whose land is this?" Once you have identified the answer to that question, begin to publicly and regularly acknowledge during your worship the violence that has been done to the land and to the indigenous people from whom it was taken whether through genocide or unfair or broken treaties. Then, initiate steps to take responsibility for that ongoing injustice through material acts of reparation and care for the earth.

2. Form a small, diverse group of persons to conduct a study of your worship space in which you audit all images, symbols, and texts that are present throughout your immediate worship space and, if applicable, entire building. What races and racial histories are materially visible and present? Which races or racial histories are less represented, not represented at all, or represented in demeaning ways? Identify practical steps that must be taken to ensure that the images, symbols, and texts in your church's space disrupt white dominance and white normativity and center other races and racial histories.

3. Develop a strategic plan to increase your community's awareness and knowledge of non-Christian religious traditions, particularly religions primarily practiced by persons who are racially minoritized, for example, Hinduism, Sikhism, Buddhism, and Islam. Taking great care to avoid appropriation and to participate in mutual dialogue, intentionally invite interreligious practitioners and incorporate interreligious sources into your worship, and, as appropriate to mutual hospitality, be responsive to invitations to enter into non-Christian spaces and, if applicable, respectfully participate in non-Christian worship.

4. For participants and leaders of white worship, educate yourself about how your racial identity within the dominant hierarchy of whiteness uniquely shapes your worship. Consult critical sources at the intersection of race and worship (start with the sources noted in the footnotes from this contribution and the entire volume) that will help you begin to glimpse how your worship is racialized, for example, white worship, and how that functions in relationship to economic, political, and social injustice along racial lines. As you learn from racially nondominant perspectives on worship, work to articulate points of consonance and points of dissonance from your experience of racially dominant white worship. Taking care to avoid appropriation, consider how you can begin to let racially nondominant liturgical images, symbols, texts, and practices critique and reshape your assumptions about worship.

5. Over the course of an extended period of time, intentionally observe what is said and unsaid in the context of your worship about racial inequity and eruptions of racial violence. During that same time period document any material actions taken by your congregation that are explicitly and intentionally anti-racist. Evaluate your findings.

Does your worship lead you and your community into consistent, tangible expressions of anti-racism? If your answers are negative, make concrete plans to consistently name race, racialized violence, and racial inequity in your worship. Commit to developing an anti-racist agenda manifested in consistent, material actions that disrupt racism in your community.

INTERCULTURAL WORSHIP

Safwat Marzouk, associate professor of Hebrew Bible/Old Testament,
Anabaptist Mennonite Biblical Seminary

About sixty years ago, Martin Luther King Jr. said in an interview, "I think it is one of the tragedies of our nation, one of the shameful tragedies, that eleven o'clock on Sunday morning is one of the most segregated hours, if not the most segregated hours, in Christian America. I definitely think the Christian church should be integrated, and any church that stands against integration and that has a segregated body is standing against the spirit and the teachings of Jesus Christ, and it fails to be a true witness."[1] For the most part, these words still ring true. Many churches are functioning under a monocultural mindset in which a particular ethnic or cultural worldview is taken for granted and whoever wishes to join this congregation is welcome as long as they assimilate into the fold. Other churches function under the model of multicultural mindset in which cultural and ethnic differences are welcomed and celebrated, but for the most part different people and their cultures are integrated in worship and leadership only occasionally or symbolically. What King called for was integration not representation. This vision we now call "intercultural church and worship." While multiculturalism is about coexistence, interculturalism, argue Agnes Brazal and Emmanuel De Guzman "not only respects difference but creates a space for the interaction of diverse cultural groups within a society" and for our purposes here, a church.[2]

I was invited to preach at a church on a Sunday that was dedicated to "mission." The topic was left open, so I decided to preach on the theme of a biblical vision for the church to become more intercultural. This may sound like a far-off topic to preach on a mission Sunday. Mission, some would assume, has to do with going out to the world, somewhere far in the Southern Hemisphere to preach the gospel. But that was precisely what I wanted to challenge. What if we think about the gathered faith community around the word and sacraments to worship God through word and body as an essential part of God's mission. If we accept this point, then the next question is, what are we embodying about God's mission in the world in relation to the diversity of the church when we gather to worship? I believe that in a world that is polarized by politics, in a world that is divided by acts of injustice, worshipping God with people who are different from us, and worshipping God in ways and in languages that make us uncomfortable, is an embodied witness for God's reconciling mission in the world.

Worshipping God in ways that are culturally, linguistically, and theologically diverse should not be seen as a posture that is informed by political correctness. Nor should it be seen as a good response to the ever-growing racial and ethnic diversity in North American society. Nor should it be a survival tactic for churches that are dying. Instead, this is God's eschatological vision for the church. By eschatological, I do not mean the end of days. By eschatological, I mean God's ways of breaking into our world through the gospel of Jesus Christ to heal this broken world. That through Jesus God is creating a diverse worshipping community was the good news that the weeping John received in his vision in Revelation 5–7.

In these chapters, the book of Revelation discloses one of the most significant aspects about those who proclaim Jesus as Lord. The diverse faith community, in John's vision, sings a new song of adoration to God and the Lamb, Jesus Christ. The lyrics of their new song are this: "You are worthy to take the scroll and to open its seals, for you were slain and by your blood you purchased for God persons from every tribe, language, people, and nation. You made them a kingdom and priests to our God, and they will reign on earth" (Revelation 5:9-10).

In this song they proclaim that they do not belong to Caesar, lord of the Roman Empire; instead, they belong to God, and Jesus is their Lord, for they were ransomed by the precious blood of the Lamb. The identity of this community is marked by a unity centered around the gospel of Jesus Christ, but this unity celebrates and integrates linguistic, ethnic, and cultural diversity. Although they are singing one song, their differences are still recognizable. When this community lives up to this vision they reflect the new realities of God's reign, which is different from the empire that seeks to eliminate people's unique and distinctive cultures. Although this song is new, it employs a traditional language (Exodus 19:1-6) giving it a new meaning in order to widen the circle of God's family.

This countercultural posture of the church that integrates diversity is analogous to the Exodus narrative that is alluded to in the phrase "you have made them a kingdom and priests to our God" (Revelation 5:10; see also Exodus 19:5-6). This phrase recalls God's covenant with the people of Israel after their exodus from Egypt. In the exodus narrative God liberated the Israelites from their servitude to Pharaoh, into their service or worship to God. That is, God's redemption in Exodus and God's redemption in Revelation are all about forming a worshipping community that is liberated from oppression and hegemony. Thus, the worshipping community is called to be liberated from assuming that its tradition or style of worship is the only way to worship God. Worship is essentially about God. That does not mean that our particular cultural ways of worshipping are not important. They are. But they should not be an obstacle toward integrating other languages, traditions, and styles of worship so that we may reflect God's vision for the church.

The vision of Revelation 4–7 is full of words of praise and adoration. The songs that are offered to God and the Lamb speak of God's sovereignty, glory, and power (Revelation 5:9-10, 12-13; 7:10-17). Since the book was written for a persecuted community, one finds an important window for pain and suffering to be fully present in the midst of these wonder-filled visions. Those who were persecuted are given a space to cry out to God: "How long?" (6:10). An intercultural church integrates different spiritualities, those of praise and those of lament. An intercultural worship is the worship in which praise is not the only faithful way to respond to God and to the world all around. In light of trauma of migration, racism, homophobia, and sexism, people who come to worship together from different ethnic, cultural, and linguistic backgrounds need to feel empowered to cry out together in worship, to lament, and to bear the burden together. When the church praises God, it proclaims its trust that God is sovereign to bring justice and healing to this broken world; when the church offers prayers of lament, the church becomes an agent of doing justice in the world by lifting up the voices of those who have been alienated.

When I went to preach at the church that I referred to earlier, something interesting happened that may seem trivial, but is telling. I walked into the church building and when I tried to find a pew to sit on, I was told that this spot belongs to someone else. If we are unable to give up our spot on a church pew, it will be hard to integrate different languages, cultures, and other embodied forms of worship. A church and a worship will not become intercultural if all that we try to do is to preserve tradition. Becoming an intercultural church and engaging in an intercultural worship is not opposed to or against tradition. Intercultural worship begins with understanding the worship practices and traditions of a particular context. That should be followed by naming the contribution of this worship tradition to the Christian life and also by naming how any church that cherishes this tradition could grow deeper in faith by adapting from other worship traditions. Looking around among the members of the congregation, it's important to reflect on the assumed or dominant worship tradition and as the church does that it is essential to reflect on how members of the nondominant culture have been assimilated into the dominant culture. The church, then, can take on the hard work of integrating the worship traditions of the church members who speak a different language, who would rather—if they are in their home culture—worship differently. Learning a new song in a different language or from a different cultural context is an important start. Translating the sermons or preaching in a different style helps toward integration. Eating meals together after Communion deepens the sense of fellowship. But what is more important is understanding the stories that are represented in the pews and around the table. In other words, intercultural worship is not about singing a spiritual without understanding the story of the African American community. Singing a song in Spanish is a good start, but it must be followed by understanding Hispanic cultures and by advocating for integrating this community in church and social spaces. When we sit on a different pew, when we sing a new song, when we praise in a different language, when we lament in a different bodily posture, when we listen to the stories of others who are different from us, not only do we embody God's hope for a divided world, we also encounter a glimpse of God's vision for the church.

Questions and Exercises

1. Every church has a culture. Culture here means the way you do things. What is the culture of your church when it comes to worship and worship planning? Is your worship usually planned-out or spontaneous? How long is your worship time? Is the music traditional or contemporary? What are the instruments used in worship? Does your worship rely heavily on words spoken and heard? Does your worship engage the body, senses, and emotions? Why do you do worship the way you do?

2. Does your church and worship assume a dominant culture where all are welcome as long as they subscribe to the culture of worship, which usually is equated with the identity of the congregation? Does your church include people from different linguistic and cultural backgrounds and are they occasionally and symbolically represented in worship? Is your church active in transforming its worship practices in order to create spaces for all people who are present in the congregation, and is your church committed to integrating with these people no matter how hard change is?

3. Is there a migrant community that worships in your congregation building but you have had little or no interaction at all with them? What would it take to reach out to their leadership and envision cross-cultural interactions between the first-generation migrants and your church? What would it take to do Sunday school and youth groups together as a way of preparing the church to become more intercultural?

THE CALL FOR AFRICAN AMERICAN WORSHIP

The Black church's role in and relationship with the African American community has a complicated history. From its origins as a space of refuge and resistance, to being the central site of liberation movements, to present questions of commitments to its African roots, the Black church's existence has been an ever-evolving progression in the ever-evolving Black religious experience in America. The Africans who were brought to America had a myriad of religious beliefs and practices, including the belief in a transcendent, benevolent God who created the universe and was its ultimate Provider. While there are many different thoughts regarding how much of the African religious beliefs and practices survived both the Middle Passage and the effects of slavery, what can be noted is that the progression of African American religion has been nuanced and has shaped Christianity to meet the unique social context of African American life.[1]

As the Black church's role has evolved over centuries, and questions of its relevance for the community today is and continues to be valid critique of the church, African American worship has also evolved in style, ecumenical diversity, and function; however, the one constant that can be noted through the centuries is African American worship's central role in the religious expression of African American Christian life. Derived from practices that started in the deep woods or "hush harbors" in what was once called "stealing the meeting" due to its secretive nature, worship for enslaved Africans in America was essential to spiritual survival for a community sharing in the same religious experience.[2] The very origins of African American worship were communal spaces of hope and spiritual liberation, in which the communities came together, worshipping the God who was for them the great creator and liberator, and they held on to the hope that one day God would liberate them.

This core of African American worship as a source of hope and liberation is viable and necessary for African Americans who share in a common historical taproot forged in an enduring identity of African American Christianity for diasporic people displaced by the unconscionable and insidious slave trade.[3] In times when racial injustices are inflicted upon Black and Brown bodies in America, African American worship invites the participation of these marginalized and oppressed bodies into communion with God and God's people, to praise God for divine hope in something greater than the evils of this world, and becomes an expression of God's redemptive and humanizing love. This is not to say that African American worship is monolithic and functioning in the same way in every Black church in America. However, the legacy of African American worship offers the foundation for worship that is rooted in the survival and wholeness of the community, celebration of identity and personhood, and divine hope and liberation. African American worship that faithfully responds to God's call worshipfully walks with and redeems the oppressed.

Often characterized by its celebratory nature, embodied experience, and rich connection between the sacred and the secular (born out of the African worldview), African American worship has been and continues to be a place where the story of our existence in the light of God's power and grace can be told. In telling those stories through music, prayer, and soul-stirring preaching, the Black church has a moral responsibility and accountability for the lives of the community, and our interconnection that makes us whole. This interconnection is rooted in a perception of kinship, where there is a concomitant valuing of one another, a common ground marked by trust, respect, and care. This communal responsibility comes with its complexities, but ever since the secret meetings of African slaves in North America, it has been integral to African American life and worship. In his work *Slave Religion*, Albert Raboteau describes this strong communal support for early African American worship: "Prayer, preaching, song, communal support, and especially 'feeling the spirit' refreshed the slaves and consoled them in their times of distress. By imagining their lives in the context of a different future they gained hope in the present."[4] Through various ritual practices, African American worship enlivens the imagination of the worshipper beyond the oppressive social structures imposed by the dominant culture, and generates anti-structures, which are alternative ways of relating to society at large. The power of this communal focus, or kinship approach, should inform African American worship practices toward building the mutuality of love and respect. Worship leaders should seek to lead in a way that is a reminder that those gathered in worship are part of God's creation, as individuals and collectively; that they belong to a divine family or community. When we *re-member* the community and remind individuals of their connectedness to God and one another through our worship, we subvert the harmful dehumanizing impact of oppression, an impact that seeks to isolate and devalue marginalized persons.

This interrelatedness in and through worship is essential in the hard reality of African American life that is still filled with extreme measures of injustice and violence against Black bodies in America. Within the last decade, the increased visibility and explicitly violent and deadly nature of racism against the African American community has presented questions of the Black church's role and relevance in response to the social climate. Many have found the church to be silent, or inactive, and movements like Black Lives Matter challenged the church's presence and action in protest against social and political injustices. The clarion call from social justice movements and advocates has been a call for the Black church to become partners of the movement. This challenge brings a very real urgency for worship in the Black church to be embodied in ways that reach beyond the walls of a sanctuary. This happens as worshipping communities engage the foot soldiers of protests, by showing up and being present in inner cities, and by recognizing that liturgical practice can happen even in the moments outside of traditional worship settings.

In her book *Faith and Ferguson: Sparking Leadership and Awakening Community*, Leah Gunning Francis recounts the protests following the death of Michael Brown and the ways many clergy leaders became involved in the community's protest. Her book opens with this illustration:

> On September 29, a typical protest night took a memorable turn. Young activists were present and chanting fervently, and the police were posted in front of them, fully dressed in riot gear. However,

on this day, more clergy were present than usual. . . . In the midst of the standoff, a few clergy took a decidedly different public action: they knelt on the sidewalk outside the police station and prayed. They symbolically laid their collars on the altar of justice and made clear that their resistance was an action of their faith.[5]

For several weeks following the heinous murder of George Floyd on May 25, 2020, liturgies of lament and protest were held in cities across the country (in addition to massive riots). Congregations gathered—wearing masks and remaining physically distanced to adhere to COVID-19 safety guidelines—to pray, sing, and mourn the violence of this country. Anti-racism–centered worship services permeated digital platforms and told the stories of the community.

The responsibility and power of African American worship in these times of heightened social trauma, and in the everydayness of life, is to create spaces of lament, as well as celebrate the humanity of the dehumanized community members, to preach the relevant gospel that challenges the evil of society, and to move beyond the safe and common spaces and practices and imagine a deeper connection with the community. African American worship, rooted in divine love and justice, recognizes and names those on the margins, and it tells the story of the community in the light of God's power and grace, moving the center of the liturgical paradigm to the margins. It embraces and is led by the dynamic presence of the Holy Spirit as a source of survival and triumph for marginalized bodies, which gifts the worshipper a real and present spiritual liberation, one that calls some to social action, others to ministerial leadership, and some to give encouraging words to the community. African American Christian worship can allow every physical body to freely express itself in the presence of the One who cares about their humanity;[6] and Black bodies can experience themselves as beloved in Christ. African American worship that exists in the sanctuaries and in the trenches of social resistance does so with the anticipation of encountering the divine intersection of life and faith.

Questions and Exercises

1. Take a moment and think about the deep connection of African American worship to the lived experiences of the community. What is your perception of ways that the worship leaders in your context relate the components of worship (music, preaching, praying, etc.) to real-life situations? Are these ways related to current local and global events? Name the last time there was an explicit intersection of lived experience in your worship service.

2. Reflect on the last ten years of racial violence inflicted on African American people, particularly at the hands of law enforcement. How did your congregation respond in worship? Were there rituals practiced within your congregation that created community and held space for these experiences? For example, testimony is a way of naming the struggles and triumphs of the past and present that transforms the gathered into a

covenant community. When have you seen these transformative rituals outside of the traditional worship spaces?

3. What are intentional ways in which your worship empowers the connection and value of community, beyond just being together in the space to worship? How are your worship practices making visible marginalized bodies?

ASIAN AMERICAN CONSIDERATIONS

In the introduction to *Worship on the Way,* Russell Yee, in the first book-length treatment of Asian American worship and still the only monograph of its kind at the time of this writing, begins by asking the reader where might one go to find expressions of Asian North American (ANA) culture. A wedding banquet? A history museum? Cultural artifacts from ANA writers, artists, filmmakers, architects, and musicians? Asian American academic departments in universities, research and writing about Asian American identity? A street fair, parade, cultural center, health care clinic, immigration center? The career of an ANA politician, athlete, or online in various forums? After painting a pastiche of possibilities, Yee writes, "Unfortunately, one of the places you are not likely to seek a particularly full and deep expression of ANA identity and culture is an ANA Christian Church."[1] Yee notes that whether the congregation is bilingual, multilingual, or predominantly English speaking, with the exception of a potluck lunch following the service, "by and large you will find forms of worship that are more closely tied to the majority culture than to anything identifiably ANA."[2] The homogenization of Asian American worship to what Yee calls the majority culture (and here what we would identify as white mainline Protestant and evangelical forms of worship) still remains prevalent. It suggests the need for more pioneering and signature approaches to Asian American Christian worship.

For example, diasporic Chinese communities have developed in-house music ministry and music publishing arms, such as Streams of Praise Music Ministries (**讚美之泉**), that offer Mandarin-language praise songs with circulation not only in the United States but also in Canada, Europe, Panama, Taiwan, Hong Kong, Australia, New Zealand, Singapore, and Malaysia. Yet the musicality, though drawing upon Taiwanese pop, still largely takes its cues from Christian Contemporary Worship Music publishing houses such as Maranatha! Music and Hosanna! Music and the Hillsong catalog, according to Swee Hong Lim and Lester Ruth.[3] While Asian American worship cannot be reduced to musical expression, music is often a third of the entire worship service in an evangelical setting. Most Asian Americans are evangelical Protestant.[4] It has been reported that "Asian-American evangelical Protestants rank among the most religious groups in the U.S., surpassing white evangelicals in weekly church attendance (76% vs. 64%)."[5] Therefore, the adoption of white evangelical music making with dynamic equivalence shows just how permeating "majority culture" is when it comes to Asian American worship. Facets of worship in Asian

American campus ministries may hint at emerging forms of Asian American worship, especially with regard to the particular content of prayers, proclamations, and some ritualizing. Yet the overall pattern in those groups still bears resemblance to the song-proclamation-response three-part structure of evangelical worship.

There are, however, some elements of Asian American worship that are idiomatic. Take for example the prayer form of *Tongsung kido* ("praying together aloud"). The words *tong* and *sung* (*seong*) are derived from the Mandarin Chinese characters 通聲, which can be rendered in English as "all sound."[6] *Tongsung kido* is a prayer form practiced in Korean and Korean American churches as well as many congregations across Asia where congregants are invited to pray simultaneously and aloud to God even if the particular content of their prayers differs. The prayer concludes as the leader's voice quiets. In *Worship for the Whole People of God*, Ruth Duck reports how Myungsil Kim, a teacher in Korean seminaries, found that *tongsung kido* likely began as lament against the harsh rule of Japan.[7] Channeling Kim, Duck continues:

> It was a way that people poured out their anguish to a comforting God and expressed lament, as in the psalms of Israel and the words of Jesus on the cross. She argues that Tongsung kido can serve worship in and beyond Korean traditions, wherever people are suffering and have deep prayers to bring before a loving God. Kim also found that female images of God in the Hebrew Bible, ancient Israel, and the Gospels are often associated with situations that call forth lament.[8]

One Korean prayer practice adopted in the American context, however, does not amount to much that is liturgically distinct within Asian American worshipping communities.

What further complicates arriving at a solid shape for Asian American worship is the sheer variety of those who identify as Asian American and the myriad of biases and prejudices applied toward them. Many associate Asian American Christianity with Korean American Christianity and the church cultures of greater metropolitan areas including and surrounding New York, San Francisco, or Los Angeles. Yet Asian American Christian worship thrives in Starkville, Mississippi, and Tamil-speaking Lutherans worship together in Troy, Michigan, and in all states in the continental US and beyond it.[9] Asian American Christians are adopted and of mixed race, sometimes in ways that defy simple biological arithmetic. Regrettably, whether one is identified as Asian or not often depends upon how foreign-looking they are, instead of close engagement with the variety of those American people who identify as Asian and recognition of just how plural Asian American identity is.

Indeed, the reliance upon white evangelical and mainline norms by Asian Americans could be interpreted as assimilation in response to constant stigmatization with perpetual foreigner status, even if an Asian American individual or community has American heritage that goes back generations. At the time of this writing, anti–Asian American racism is rampant due to public associations of a pandemic virus as "Chinese." The absence of distinguishable and shared idiomatic practices of Asian American worship may also indicate an unconscious liturgical protective measure to buffer against discrimination against Asian American peoples.

Furthermore, the plurality of Asian American identity destabilizes any attempt to reach a consensus regarding what Asian American Christianity actually is. And worship is not often ready to wrestle with such complexity or find ways to celebrate and embrace it through Christian prayer, ritual, proclamation, and song. Such plurality also includes stark political differences that result in clashing over issues such as abortion, same-sex marriage, and the ordination of LGBTQIA+

ministers, to name a few. In a sermon based upon John 4:4-42 titled "Women on the Way," Eunjoo Mary Kim asks, "Should Asian patriarchal culture and tradition, embedded in Asian and Asian American churches, continue to be the norm in the practice of the Christian faith?"[10] Considering the goods of Asian American Christianity for worship leadership requires what Viet Thanh Nguyen calls "a theoretical framework that can address Asian America's ideological diversity and contradictions."[11] There is a historical problem in the US of treating Asian Americans as an "indistinguishable group" rather than an "aggregate of individuals."[12] Many church-friendly folks who are not of Asian descent associate Asian American Christianity with East Asian identity, and more specifically, Korean American Christianity. Yet Asian American identity is sprawling.

It requires constant recalibration and reconceptualization. Asian American Christian worship exhibits signs of domestication and diaspora that do not always cohere culturally. For example, the expansion of what we consider Asian American Christian worship to be must include questioning the prevalence of white mainline and evangelical liturgical performativity and acknowledgment of South Asian churches that are Tamil-speaking. Conversely, Asian American Christian worship must also think about the twists and turns of liturgical assimilation and change as seen, for example, in predominantly white evangelical congregations hiring lead Korean American pastors.[13] Given the multiple permutations of Asian American identity and how Asian American worship comes to expression, and the relative scarcity of idiomatic Asian American worship practices, we see exponential opportunities for leaders of Asian American assemblies and their participants to innovate and celebrate the vast and intricate dimensions of Asian American identity liturgically.

Questions and Exercises

1. In addition to post-worship potlucks that serve Asian cuisine, celebrating the Lunar New Year, inserting a hymn in an Asian language, or reading from scripture in an Asian-language translation, what are other ways in which Asian American participants in your worship service can be consulted to bring liturgical gifts?

2. If your congregation has a historical basis in diasporic Asian identity, how can worship not only preserve elements of the "home culture" but also tread new liturgical pathways for the next generation and generations to come? In other words, how can your style of worship not only transmit the goods of Asian culture, but distinctively define Asian American worship going forward?

3. In addition to having an English-language service or diversifying the congregational identity of the church, how can defining Asian American Christian worship become a shared and ongoing project of liturgical innovation? If there are so few elements of

idiomatic Asian American worship, how can that scarcity become an opportunity for liturgical ingenuity?

4. Asian Americans are described as the most educated and upwardly mobile of immigrant classes in the United States. Yet this picture distorts the extreme range of economic privilege and disadvantage represented across Asian American peoples. It also reinforces the caricature of Asian Americans as a model minority deserving of integration into Christian worship. Begin instead with thinking about how to cherish Asian Americans as family members in God whose presence and participation are crucial and necessary no matter what they bring to the table.

5. We are called to love our neighbors as ourselves. How might we embrace the "foreign-ness" of Asian American identity as an encounter with another image of God and as an opportunity to extend selfish love charitably in the name of God? How might we resist stereotypes about what constitutes Asianness (karate, Bruce Lee, Jackie Chan, the exotic and docile temptress, and misplaced questions regarding place of origin for example) with the same kind of privileging love we apply to ourselves (in our most mentally healthy state) so that Asian American Christian worship is seen not as an outlier or something to be absorbed in mainstream American Christian culture, but a nascent liturgical expression in which we delight and find out more about who we are in God?

We have witnessed the pitfalls of pastors, presidents, and deans who attempt to institute diversity programming without having relationships with diverse peoples in their own lives. Consider the imaginary example of an institution that seeks to address its slave legacy or Black Lives Matter with deep molecular change when it has never had a black pastor, president, or dean, and where the current leadership has never had black bosses, teachers, or friends. The imaginative leap seems tremendous, even outrageous. Before nurturing Christian worship capable of serving diverse peoples, we recommend cultivating a coherence between personal piety and wider liturgical aspirations in order to establish theological integrity. Without substantive relationships with persons of differing abilities, color, gendered and sexual identities, and other political markers, the reflection and work we recommend will likely risk hypocrisy or remain liturgically shallow. How can a worship leader facilitate diverse worship without having diverse friendships? All it takes to begin building more coherence between private and public devotional spheres is loving our neighbors as ourselves.

INTERGENERATIONAL CHURCH TODAY AND TOMORROW

If a church is not already filled with persons under the age of forty (and even when it is), a primary question that we often hear asked is "How do we keep young people interested in church?" The question, however, sees the vitality of worship with concern only for how to reach the young and inculcate them into the existing life of the church. Over the past few years in the academy, I have advised doctor of ministry students with research focused on millennials and the church in one way or another, whether it was preaching to millennials, getting millennials more involved in the church, or even getting them to show up. In doing this work, I have found that there is quite a bit of research offered and interest in communities to appeal to the younger generations on the basis of growing the church and establishing longevity and legacy. The only twist is, millennials are no longer young, or are "youngish" at best. The eldest millennials are now middle aged. Therefore, ministering to the young in Christian worship requires constant liturgical review and refashioning. In order to do this, we turn our emphasis and efforts toward recruiting and retaining younger persons in our communities, which at the time of this writing compose Generation Z. But we'll need to be ready for generations beyond that last letter of the alphabet too. Yet most important, we should instead ask how to nurture an ecology of worship that appeals to all ages and finds wisdom in the dynamic relationships between generations.

Active church participants are aging faster than the American population.[1] Clergy across mainline churches are aging faster than the US population;[2] and statistics show that as the Silent Generation is close to dying out, Baby Boomers tend to be the most consistent worship attendees followed by Generation X and then millennials.[3] This imbalance not only provides rationale for injecting new (and younger) blood into the church, it also suggests that there are years of wisdom worth sharing across generations in worship. This reality provides great creative opportunities for worship to include younger persons in worship leadership, developing a space for them to glean from the experience of those from older generations, while also offering their gifts, wisdom, and youthful passion. Actions like this might (and should) transform the tone, emphasis, and even energy of worship. This also might invite more insightful dialogue around matters of worship by way of preparation and reflection. What does it look like to hold small group worship conversations led by two persons from different age groups? How might the inclusion of youth and young adults in worship leadership change the congregation's worship imagination?

An intergenerational approach or focus in worship will inevitably bring about communal transformation that allows organic connection and church growth. It provides a place of investment and connection for all generations—including those emerging into adulthood, as well as those deemed old. It moves beyond siloed services that celebrate particular ages and enlivens the rich history and vibrant future of the church to converge in worshipful ways. However, it is to be noted that this type of worship environment takes careful planning and time. It requires educational moments that intentionally celebrate and publicly value the gathered generations of the community. It is more than just adding youth to the sanctuary and proceeding with worship as usual. It is more than just allowing younger persons to read a scripture (although this is a good place to start). The idea is to create space for all generations to actively worship together, with their whole selves. This requires reimagining communal worship altogether. It is not dumbing down services and sermons, rather hearing what is relevant and real to all who are gathered and allowing that to intersect in worship. It calls for hearing from all ages, experimenting (even when it is uncomfortable), and a willingness to be flexible.

Case Study

Growing into Intergenerational Worship—A Pastor's Perspective

The Reverend Dr. Damon P. Williams was a 31-year-old pastor who answered the call to lead a 141-year-old historic Baptist church in 2012. At the onset of his pastorate, the church was thriving, yet the average age of the congregation was sixty to sixty-five years old, and the need, desire, and urgency to integrate younger generations was high. At the start, Williams admits he knew that worship would be appealing to the older adults in the church, but what was happening in worship probably would not be appealing or inviting to the youth and young adults of the church. Thinking about how to facilitate intergenerational worship was a large conversation in the church. But implementing intergenerational worship was not actually happening. The first step in his efforts was to build relationships and converse with the younger members of the church in order to find out what they were looking for in the worship experience—what would make them feel included, seen, and heard. What he found was a desire to be included and to be authentic. They wanted to be included in the leadership and worship decisions, and they wanted the freedom to be fully themselves in the process.

Over the years, Reverend Williams and his congregation have worked to implement a number of changes to integrate younger persons into the worship rhythm of the church that included having youth sit in the pulpit. Williams says this was a huge first step in his congregation. Youth began to participate in worship by reading scripture, offering the welcome, assisting during Communion, and eventually delivering a sermon on a designated Sunday in the month. The church has invited more laypersons of all ages into the worship leadership, and took time to be in conversation with many members of the congregation, from the eldest to the youngest, through this initiative in order to hear from everyone. In these conversations, they found there were points of synergy from which they could build, and the more the groups heard from one another, the more they were willing to experience the different ways of worshipping that were not necessarily their preference. While he admits there is still work to be done, Reverend Williams is excited they have created an environment in which youth and young adult presence in worship is a natural part of their ethos, and not just reserved for special Sundays or occasions. While they still have separate services for the youth of the church, it is now a norm within worship to have diverse age groups leading in a service. Here are a few lessons Reverend Williams shared from this work:

1. Demystify the pulpit.

Williams found that much of the resistance to intergenerational worship came from those who held the notion that the pulpit was reserved only for clergy. This thought created a power dynamic that limited who was able to be in the pulpit. Demystifying this space and making it more inclusive to all persons was a major hurdle in getting more traditional members to become comfortable and even accepting of non-clergy members in worship leadership.

2. Initiate intergenerational conversation about worship.

Get all of the voices in the space together and let them define worship for themselves. Find out what worship means for them. A good place to start these conversations is within small family groups. Explore how the different age groups experience the Holy in worship. Then identify the points of synergy in the ways that different generations experience and understand God. Let those points of synergy inform your worship transformation, and invite the generations to build it together.

3. Make room for youth and laypersons to lead in their own way or style.

In moving into intergenerational worship, Williams admits that even he had to reimagine how worship looked and felt. It was important to not ask youth, young adults, and laypersons to try and fit into a traditional box in their leadership, but to create the space and environment that gave them the freedom to be themselves and lead in the way they were most comfortable. This was particularly important for the youth, as it helped them cultivate confidence in who they are and what they are capable of doing.

4. Take your time in the transition, while also being bold.

Congregational change takes time. In eight years of doing this work, Reverend Williams still sees room for continued growth toward fully intergenerational worship. Being patient and willing to make bold steps toward transformation are key. Every decision will not be immediately popular, but they should be pastoral.

Questions and Exercises

1. Churches often host special age-related worship services such as Youth Sunday. What would it look like to more intentionally structure worship according to different stages of life associated with age and to think how to blend the challenges and the blessings of different life stages? For example, what does a service look like when it pairs the confusion, awkwardness, exhilaration, and adventure of adolescence with the confusion, sorrow, wisdom, and grace of old age?

2. If everyone is made in the image of God, how might we look to every person at every age as a living icon, or as a living scripture, portraying who God is for us? What would it entail to contemplate the faces, bodies, and experiences of every child, adolescent, and adult in all of their glory and frailty as individuals worthy of contemplation who disclose knowledge of God that can inspire any act of worship?

3. Children and young people are often invited to share special music. Churches also frequently feature a "children's moment." In addition to those service elements, or instead of them, invite a child and young person to preach. Some church traditions do so with regularity and as a form of spiritual mentorship. If the child or young person is nervous about offering a message alone, propose the option of preaching with another friend or as a team.

4. Bring together a focus group of different-aged members of your congregation to think about intergenerational worship. Ask them to commit to a series of conversations that will help inform the future of your congregation's worship. Hear their stories of what is most valuable to them in worship, and what they don't care for. Invite them to listen to one another and to identify points of similarities. The goal of the conversations is to develop worship relationships among the group, and then to identify how this group can help build a new way of worshipping. Do a number of these conversations with a few different groups over the course of a year, as you actively live into intergenerational worship.

Chaplaincy: Reimagining Hospital Rituals in the Context of COVID-19

Emily Lueder, outpatient palliative care chaplain with
Hackensack Meridian Health in New Jersey

Chaplains are often called upon to facilitate rituals and other acts of worship with patients, families, and hospital staff. As observed by sociologist Wendy Cadge, these rituals are commonly end-of-life rituals, taking the form of baptisms, blessings, or the Sacrament of the Sick as a patient draws near to death or soon after a death occurs.[1] They typically take place at the bedside, and water or oil may be used if a formal ritual is requested. Family members or friends often, although not always, gather together in order to lay their hands on their loved one or simply hold the person's hand as an informal ritual. For those who were unable to be present, some hospitals hold memorial services to remember patients and staff who have died.[2] Each one of these end-of-life rituals and its meaning(s) are highly contextual and depend upon the patient's specific faith and values, the person's relationships with family and friend groups, and the circumstances surrounding their hospitalization, among other factors. At the same time, all of these rituals highlight the deep need for human connection in times of loss and grief. There is power in touching, in being in community, in simply being present with the patient and God or the divine.

This deeply intimate way of performing rituals at a bedside or in worshipping together in a hospital chapel has been upended, however, with the emergence of COVID-19. Communities across the nation have been forced to grapple with policies and procedures aimed at limiting its spread. Businesses, schools, and faith communities have had to close their doors and find new ways of connecting and operating safely instead. Hospitals have been no different as administrators and other leaders consider new policies regarding personal protective equipment (PPE) and visitor restrictions that seek to protect patients and staff.[3] Within some pastoral care and spiritual care departments, difficult decisions have been made that prohibit in-person visitation with patients who are thought to have or who have tested positive for the virus and embrace tele-chaplaincy as an alternative. Chaplaincy as a whole looks different in this context as chaplains are challenged to find new ways of connecting with patients and families to offer emotional and spiritual support and continue facilitating meaningful rituals in different, sometimes disembodied, ways.

Consider, for example, that the most tangible elements of these bedside rituals have essentially been stripped away for the sake of infection prevention. The chaplains, who typically serve as "the visible, present, professional carriers of religion and spirituality in hospitals," can no longer enter these patients' rooms and signal the beginning of a ritual with their very presence.[4] Rather, some are relegated to the hallways of busy intensive care units (ICUs), often reciting prayers and performing blessings and anointings outside of patient doors as the care teams work around them. Others harness available technology, most often iPads or tablets, to preserve the intimacy inherent to these moments with patients and families near and far as much as possible. In either case, the chaplain is no longer embodied in the traditional and expected way. Likewise, the other symbolic elements—the water, the oil, the laying-on of hands—are noticeably absent at the bedside, too. These stripped down, on-the-fly rituals now demand enactment in other ways and with different symbolic elements.

Paradoxically, as stay-at-home orders were issued, social distancing measures encouraged, and visitor restrictions announced, images of community became a powerful symbol upon which chaplains could and can draw during rituals with patients and families. If technology is available, chaplains may invite the patient's family to participate in these rituals, to hold out their hands through FaceTime or Zoom and pray along with the chaplain, but more can be done with this image. In the Spiritual Assessment and Intervention Model used by some chaplains to assess the spiritual needs of patients, chaplains are encouraged to acknowledge or name what is happening in the room. Most often, this takes the form of naming feelings or relational dynamics that are observed at the bedside.[5] But, naming can also be a part of rituals, even virtual rituals. Chaplains can name the pain and anger that emerge when families and friends cannot be with their dying loved one. They can also name what is happening on the screen or in the hallway before them, even drawing upon the patient and family's faith tradition as a lens. For a Christian patient and family, for example, the chaplain could name the assurance of Christ's presence "where two or three are gathered in [his] name" (Matthew 18:20 NRSV). In doing so, the family not only participates in the ritual through praying, naming, or some other action, but also serves as a symbol for something greater within the ritual.

As these rituals are reimagined in light of COVID-19 restrictions, the accompanying liturgy can also be reimagined to give expression to the profound loss and grief that come with this particular crisis. In an interview for the American Psychological Association, psychologist Kiersten Weir discusses the potential "sense of ambiguous loss" experienced by people who cannot be present for their loved one's death or grieve that loss in community. She notes that there can be "a lot of frustration and helplessness, because people feel disempowered."[6] This, too, can be named by the chaplain if and when she or he gathers with the patient and family for a ritual, but it can also be incorporated into the liturgy for the ritual. Ideally, then, the liturgy would create space for the patient and family to express these feelings and simply lament. This can be done with the help of traditional prayers, like the Lord's Prayer or the Hail Mary, and extemporaneous prayers that draw upon images and verses from scripture. The Psalms are an especially helpful resource for helping patients and families to lament. At the same time, the liturgy would ideally offer some possibility for hope and healing that can guide the family forward. Again, this hope can be incorporated into the liturgy through prayers and familiar images depending on the faith tradition of the patient and family. It is ultimately a delicate balancing act that demands creativity, sensitivity, and wisdom on the part of the chaplain.

At the time of this writing, it is unclear when COVID-19 will be a thing of the past, if it ever will be at all. It seems likely that chaplains will be reimagining rituals with patients and their families for the foreseeable future. This reframing and reimagining work will demand creativity, flexibility, and sensitivity as chaplains journey with patients and families in naming their grief and searching for a glimpse of hope and healing.

> On a quiet Thursday morning, I (Emily) responded to a request for spiritual care for the family of Juan, a man who was dying from complications related to COVID-19. Once on the unit, I was introduced to Sofia, Juan's sister and the sole family member allowed in to say her goodbyes. She primarily spoke Spanish, so Juan's nurse served as translator and verified that Sofia was Catholic and wanted a blessing for her brother in lieu of a last rite.
>
> All three of us, strangers bound together by the ravages of the pandemic, huddled together in the bustling hallway, separated from Juan by a makeshift wall. I began the blessing by lifting up the prayers that Sofia had shared with me beforehand and left space for her to name specific family members who would need to grieve alone before leading the Lord's Prayer. Sofia and the nurse then closed with the Hail Mary as I stood beside them.
>
> What was happening in the hallway may not have been traditional or expected. But it looked like a vision of Pentecost to me. It looked like a community of strangers, Spanish- and English-speaking, Catholic and Protestant, gathered together by the Holy Spirit.

Questions and Exercises

1. Rituals that used to take place primarily at the bedside have been moved elsewhere and some hospital chapels temporarily closed in order to prevent the spread of COVID-19. This has required chaplains to utilize other mundane spaces, like ICU hallways, for sacred purposes. What is it that makes a space sacred? How could a chaplain or other faith leader help a family to enter into these kinds of makeshift sacred spaces?

2. A significant part of a chaplain's training involves reflecting upon his or her own experiences and the ways in which those experiences shape the work done with patients, families, and staff. Reflect upon your own experiences with loss and grief. What end-of-life rituals have you observed in your own family or faith community? What was done

or said that was helpful or meaningful? What else would have given space to lament or pointed in the direction of hope?

3. Think about your own faith tradition. What prayers, images, or scriptures would be familiar and meaningful if you were called upon to perform an end-of-life ritual for someone from your own congregation? Sit down with someone from a different denomination, faith tradition, or no faith tradition. What would be meaningful to him or her? What resources do they lean into in times of crisis?

4. Chaplains are often present as families begin to process their loss and grief, but faith leaders and their congregations are well positioned to journey with these families throughout the whole process. How does your current liturgy make space for lament? Where could you make this space within the context of your worship?

IMBUING LITURGICAL AWE

Do you remember the last time that you said "wow" about a service? Maybe it happened recently. Was it a special service for a particular liturgical season or high holy day? Or perhaps you have not been wowed in a while, and when you have, it has not been more than a handful of times. You cherish those memories and will carry them with you. But they do not provide a point of reference to draw upon for imbuing or deeply injecting awe into the services that you lead.

> While visiting an old friend in Lausanne, Switzerland, I (Gerald) randomly stumbled with him into an Advent service of gifts led by a worldwide network of Christian musicians known as Crescendo in the Cathedral of Notre Dame of Lausanne.[1] The pattern involved a bricolage of varying artistic contributions from beatboxing to performances of the classical composer Ravel, to a famous media cartoonist testifying about his faith, all ordered in various stations where one could move throughout the sanctuary and also engage in prayer, pastoral counsel, and silent rituals with candlelight, sacred objects, and water. I had never seen anything like it and it remains the most unusual and amazing Advent service I have experienced.

If we wanted to make awe a regular feature of our worship leading, how would we go about doing it? One way that we think awe can be produced and not merely remembered or dreamed is by ensuring that a service is sensory-rich. Most worship services catch the eye, resonate within the ear, and perhaps tickle the nose and taste buds depending upon the tradition and the rites that are being celebrated. Yet how might any service of Christian worship across traditions and settings impassion all five senses?

In her book *Think Like a Filmmaker*, Marcia McFee offers a guide to intentional worship design that pays attention to all of the senses to create meaningful and memorable worship through various sensory elements including visuals, language, music, media arts, and dramatic arts (which includes all ritual action).[2] She offers a vision of worship planning or designing that gives the worshipping community an interaction and point of view they may not normally have. Through worship series based on a particular theme, McFee has witnessed communities strengthen their liturgical journey together, and found through a variety of ritual actions and intentional creative framing that communities can worship together and encounter a sense of wonder and awe.

Sensory-rich worship has the power to share the gospel message in ways the community may never have encountered before. However, it is a process that takes time. So, advance planning is key. In addition, what impacts one person is not going to be the same for everyone in the congregation. As you think through designing worship series or even stand-alone services, think creatively about your sensory engagement from one service to another. If you offer prayer stations with tangible objects for engagement to incite an embodied experience in one service, consider a different approach for the next service that does not focus on touch and movement. In a four-week worship series, you might want to consider a sensory progression from the first to the last service in which you offer one or two creative points of engagement to start with and then continue adding until the fourth service. This offers an opportunity for the unfamiliar to become familiar, while continuing to introduce something new and wonderful with each service.

If intentionally designing worship that imbues a sense of awe within the community is new for you and your congregation, then getting the word out about this liturgical journey is crucially important. Let the congregation know about the journey ahead of time and invite them into the process of preparation. Set aside the time for planning, more than you normally would, as this process takes time, especially at the beginning. Reimagine the roles of your worship team and volunteers and welcome the fullness of their gifts and creativity. Sensory-rich worship design is a collaborative process, and if you don't have a team, be open to inviting a few volunteers to act as a sounding board for you as you envision worship that is inspiring and awe-provoking.

Questions and Exercises

1. Is there a song, visual, ritual, or gift of liturgical action that you have experienced in another worship setting or conjured in your mind that you have always wanted to try in your particular context of worship leadership? What is holding you back from attempting it? What are the reasons for sharing it in order to benefit the worshipping assembly?

2. Is your worship pivoted more toward the auditory or visual? If you wanted to include elements that contributed to the fragrance of Christ or felt called to redeem the scandalous and health-hazardous associations of touch responsibly and with theological rigor, how would you go about doing it?

3. Experiment with setting up a four-week theme for your worship services (Advent or Lent are always easy seasons to start with). How can you integrate music, drama, movement, visuals, multimedia, and ritual in creative ways to heighten the experience of the worshipping community? What will make each service, and the series as a whole, memorable? Once you have brainstormed all of the ways you can use these areas of your

service for sensory-rich worship in the series of services, begin to think through one service at a time as a building block, choosing select elements of the service without causing sensory overload.

4. In what ways does a week-to-week sermon-focused approach to worship planning limit the spiritual journey for the entire congregation? How can you imagine a series-oriented approach that focuses on a specific theme enhancing the community's spiritual journey? What impact might it have for your worship planning team, or for yourself, if you are the only person, or one of few in the worship planning process? What possibilities are there for engaging the diversity of your congregation to incite wonder in the worship services?

5. In an effort toward sensory-rich worship, there is a risk of designing worship that may feel entertainment-oriented. What measures should be considered to avoid being entertainment focused, and to faithfully remain committed to engaging all of the senses as a worshipful act? How can you avoid sensory overload in your planning process and the actual worship service?

IDENTIFYING CONGREGATIONAL AND COMMUNITY GIFTS FOR WORSHIP

Over time, I have found it fulfilling to worship in services that are well planned and use the gifts of the community to bring that planning to life. While the following chapter will focus in-depth on collaborative worship planning, I want to explore the process of identifying the gifts the people of the congregation and community bring into the worship encounter. How do you find these gifts? Most apparent is identifying the people who are eager to serve in worship. These are the individuals who volunteer for the choir, ask to read scripture, or want to join the hospitality team. They willingly present their gifts and desires for service unto God through worship. While it may be easy to identify their willingness to volunteer in the worship life of the congregation, it will be important to ensure you work together to find the best places for them to serve on the worship planning team. Find out their passions and their strengths and begin to imagine how these may benefit the entirety of the community.

Everyone is not so forthcoming with their gifts and talents, and some people don't even know what gifts they can offer in worship. This is where focused efforts to recruit members of the congregation and getting to know them better become helpful. A good place to start is by communicating the need for volunteers within your congregation. Many people in the congregation are gifted and willing to share those gifts with the community; they are just waiting for the invitation. Also, take note of the talents of the members, such as when they invite you to their personal events, and invite them to share those gifts in worship. Set up designated time to have conversations with people who are interested in participating in worship, even if they are not sure what they have to offer. In most instances, you will lead them through on-the-job discernment to identify their gifts. Create a gracious space for you and the worship volunteers to grow faithfully together in worship.

If you find that someone has been volunteering in the same roles for worship for a long time, encourage them to explore something new. Sometimes volunteers can become bored or complacent, and there are a number of areas in the worship to encourage them to discover something new, and for you to have a new perspective offered within the community. Invite the current volunteers to partner with you in inviting other community members to share their gifts. Working with you in worship planning, leverage them to communicate the needs of the team, recruit volunteers, and encourage people to share their gifts in various ways in worship. However you go about identifying the gifts of the community, remember that including more people in the collaborative process is a faithful and just thing to do. It creates a more inclusive worship experience and cultivates a creative and vibrant community.

Questions and Exercises

1. What do you need as it relates to volunteers for worship? Starting with a sense of clarity in this area will help you shape how you identify the gifts in the community. Who volunteers regularly? Who never volunteers for worship leadership? How much openness does our community have for members to volunteer for worship? What members and groups within our community are not represented in the worship leadership?

2. Offer a worship ministry fair at the start of every year. Provide details of special services, worship guidelines, major things to know for the coming year, and opportunities for people to sign up to volunteer to serve in worship. Create a chart with worship dates, themes, and places to serve (i.e., reading scripture, offering prayer, singing, dancing, or designing liturgical space). Once the fair is complete, compile the volunteer information and begin inviting individuals to serve in various capacities. Not everyone will select their right fit initially. However, embrace the process of letting community members find their way, and encourage continued participation (with guidance) until the right place to serve in worship is identified. There is growth for the individual, the congregation, and the worship life in the process.

3. Create and circulate a worship resource and volunteer survey. Here is one example:

The worship planning team of our congregation aims to include the gifts and leadership of our community in worship. We believe worship is not done for the people, as though they were spectators, but *by* the people of God as their corporate offering of adoration and praise to God. We solicit volunteers of all ages and abilities, who are willing to see this participation as part of their ministry to the body of Christ. A commitment should be made for _____ *(state the amount of time desired, one year is pretty standard)*, and all volunteers will partner with and serve under the supervision of the worship planning team.

Since we begin a new list each season, please note that those who signed up last year must sign up again. If you have any questions, or if you desire a copy of our worship guidelines, please speak with a member of our worship leadership team.

Your Name: _____

Liturgy

Please check your area of interest. You may indicate multiple areas of involvement.

- ❏ I'd be willing to participate in readings, litanies, and scripture reading.
- ❏ I'd be willing to lead in readings and prayers with the Advent candles this season.
- ❏ I'd be willing to write prayers and litanies.
- ❏ I'd be willing to participate in a dramatized Scripture reading for worship.
- ❏ I'd be willing to coach an occasional Scripture drama group.
- ❏ I'd be willing to dance with the liturgical dance group in worship.
- ❏ I'd be willing to lead in prayer.
- ❏ I'd be willing to be a part of the worship planning team.
- ❏ I'd be willing to help coordinate the liturgical space.

Music—Vocal

- ❏ I'd be willing to participate as a soloist (indicate the appropriate vocal range):

  Soprano   Alto   Tenor   Bass

- ❏ I'd be willing to participate as part of a theme choir, such as a family choir, women's group, men's choir, or young adult ensemble.

Music—Instrumental

- ❏ I'd be interested in serving as an accompanist or providing an offertory.
- ❏ I'd like to be considered for the bell choir as openings become available.

Chapter 30

❏ I'm willing to participate in a small-instrumental ensemble:

Instrument(s) played _____

❏ I'm willing to serve as an instrumental soloist.

Music—Occasional Ensembles

❏ I'd be willing to participate in an ensemble:

• Middle School Vocal

• High School Vocal

• Trumpet

• Flute

• String

Music—Administration

❏ I'd be willing to serve as a music librarian.

❏ I'd be willing to serve as a music task force member.[1]

4. When members join the church, provide questions in the intake form inquiring how they would like to participate in the worship life. Once this information is received, it should be passed along to the worship leadership team and someone should reach out to follow up with the new members, welcoming them into the congregation and confirming the gifts they desire to bring to the worship life of the church.

PLANNING TOGETHER

Worship that brings our congregations into a rich awareness of God's presence requires intentional and careful worship planning. It requires commitment, creativity, and a variety of spiritual gifts that are present only in a collaborative model for planning worship. Whether it is a large church with a full staff, or a small church where the pastor does all of the heavy lifting of the day-to-day operations, collaborative worship planning is essential to honoring God's sharing of a variety of spiritual gifts among us.

Practically speaking, collaborative worship planning is a way to enhance the reach and connection of worship within congregations. For many congregations, worship happens once a week and sometimes more often. The weekly rhythm of worship every Sunday calls for dynamic worship experiences that are hard to create with only one person planning. In *Encounters with the Holy*, Barbara Day Miller recommends a shared method of worship planning she describes with the acronym POWR. Planning a worship with POWR entails distinguishing between functional aspects of worship planning—what readings and hymns should we choose, for example—and imaginative dimensions that may not always proceed in a linear way toward completing liturgical "slots" that need to be filled. Instead Day Miller suggests *planning* (here's the *P* in POWR) in a swirl of conversation that grows out of foundations like scriptural interpretation and then moves to *order* (here's the *O*) where ideas are vetted and then materialized with respect to space, elements, people, and more. Then we *worship* (here's the *W*) as a full expression of our planning and ordering. Afterward we *reflect* (here's the *R*) so that we can think about how we glorified God and celebrated the love of God and neighbor, and also so that we can keep worship robust and not routine.[1] Planning together as a team invites inclusivity, and the worship planners experience a greater sense of creativity through the expanded insight and skills, with a balance of variety. This model of planning together offers an opportunity for congregations to worship with a greater balance, variation, and creativity, given through inclusion of more voices in envisioning the service and the arc of the worship life of the congregation.

The first step in planning together is to determine who should be involved in the planning process. In *The Next Worship*, Sandra Maria Van Opstal suggests that leaders of worship need to think about how hospitality, solidarity, and mutuality are constellating, overlapping, and informing one another as ethical values privileged in shared worship planning.[2] To put it another way, for Van Opstal, planning together depends upon the exercise of reconciliation between people who may be and are hopefully very different from one another as an evolution in hospitality that churches have struggled to express historically.[3] Who are the key stakeholders and partners in worship leadership? The pastor? Music leaders? Clergy? Lay members? How do you choose who serves on the worship planning team? It takes a particular kind of savvy to understand and discern the different ways in which leadership can happen (managerially, democratically, prophetically . . .) and how to create a welcoming ecology for the different styles of communication, input, and participation that sharing leadership can involve. For Van Opstal, achieving the right balance in planning together is especially vital because "ego," "fear of failure," "control," "inefficiency," "pride/insecurity," and "self-sufficiency" can infect and unravel cohesion in group planning.[4] Or, if collaboration happens too lightly, tokenism, where the shared leadership is feigned instead of made foundational—sprinkling in a person of color in the planning process who has voice but not much influence, or adding a hymn in another language to spice things up without giving full attention to how God enriches worship with the multitude of gifts from a panorama of cultures beyond our own—is the result.

Members should, first, be chosen according to their connection to worship. The scripture and the sermon shape the entire focus for the service, even when churches follow the lectionary. In most contexts, the pastor is the central person to impact the worship planning process given that most planning is informed by the sermon; therefore, they are the starting point for assembling the worship team and will provide great insight on who else should be included. However, we recognize that some congregations have a person other than the pastor who is solely responsible for leading the worship planning process. In these situations, the minister or pastor of worship will still work closely with the pastor to create and lead the worship atmosphere. Additionally, members of the team should be chosen according to their heart for the worship planning. Consider making the team as expansive as possible, while keeping in mind the best size for team planning for your particular community. This expansive view is a matter of justly offering balanced worship.

Examples of Worship Planning Processes

Example 1—Solo Pastor Weekly Planning

A Maryland-based solo pastor leading a United Methodist congregation handles almost all of the worship planning process on her own. She has a part-time musician who assists in leading worship, and one layperson volunteer. She plans her services two weeks in advance, and the process begins with the sermon focus, which is usually based on the lectionary texts. Upon prayerfully selecting the texts for the service, she outlines the order of worship, which tends to follow the same pattern each week. She meets with the part-time musician once a week to discuss music selection and worship flow. Together they think through the flow, make note of any special or unique moments in the service, and identify volunteers needed for worship leadership. The pastor then invites volunteers where appropriate, writes liturgies for the service, and crafts her sermon (which has been in the works during the entire process). When her congregation pivoted to online worship, she began to plan three weeks ahead, but did not have any collaboration as she streamlined the services to include prerecorded music to open the service, prayer, scripture, sermon, and benediction, all of which she led.

Example 2—Planning a Series with a Full Staff

A large, African American Disciples of Christ church in Indianapolis plans worship according to a four-week series rhythm. While this does not comprise the entire year, the pastor shares that approximately 75 percent of their worship year is shaped this way. Using the full staff, he leads the worship-planning process by casting the vision of the new series two to three weeks in advance, although the team has the focus of the series six months in advance through their worship and ministries planning calendar. Once the vision is cast, the staff dedicates a portion of their weekly staff meeting to worship planning. The staff includes the senior pastor, pastor of worship and arts ministry, executive pastor, project manager, executive assistant, youth and young adult pastor, minister to women, and the minister of Christian education, among others. Once the pastor offers his overall vision for the worship series and specific services, the executive pastor and pastor of worship and arts lead the remainder of the planning process. As they move within two weeks of the service, they divide the tasks of the worship planning into smaller groups or individual responsibilities—the pastor of worship and arts takes on coordinating music and artistic expression, the youth and young adult pastor recruits youth participants if applicable, and the executive pastor manages all of the final details to ensure execution of the service. On the day of the worship service, the executive pastor leads the preparation and final details to ensure all is in place. Then the staff reflects on the service in the following staff meeting (a meeting that typically lasts three hours), and they begin the final preparations for the upcoming Sunday and the planning for the next two weeks. In this model, the team is always working on at least two services at a time.

Example 3—Planning Worship with an Online Audience in Mind

An Atlanta-based Baptist church plans worship for a mid-sized congregation with a strong focus on the online audience. The pastor is a solo pastor, who has cultivated a strong volunteer-based worship planning team comprising diverse members of the congregation (age, gifts, and length of time at the church) who plan along with him and the music director. The team plans for worship weekly, with the next two weeks on the horizon. The pastor is the center of the planning process. He begins with offering his sermon text, title, and synopsis to the team. They meet weekly, most times virtually to account for volunteers' work and home obligations. Each meeting lasts one hour in which they brainstorm music, participants, use of technology in the sanctuary, and online engagement. Once the structure of the service is identified, the online worship pastor manages all virtual engagement and recruitment for the team. The music director and senior pastor continue working closely to iron out the details for Sunday, and the other members of the worship team are assigned roles as worship leaders or recruit other members to participate where possible. The volunteer members of the team make an annual commitment to worship planning, and are required to roll off of the team after two years of service in order to rest and explore other areas to serve in the church. If they want to recommit to the team after a year, they are able to return for another rotation on the volunteer team.

Questions and Exercises

A Model for Planning Together

There are several models for planning worship, and we want to offer just one to prompt ideas of collaborative planning structures. Begin your planning process by scheduling your initial planning meeting. This meeting should be held either in person or through a video conference and last anywhere from sixty to ninety minutes. Subsequent meetings can be held virtually or in person and should also last about sixty minutes. When holding meetings virtually, we recommend video conferencing over an audio call because there is a greater connection in the planning process when you can see one another and the shared excitement or hesitations through body language and words. Here are a few proposed structures for your planning meetings.

1. Worship planning for an entire liturgical season or series, begin with these steps and then proceed to the suggestions for weekly worship services:

   a. Identify the seasonal rhythm or worship series with a smaller core group of the worship planning team. Identify the seasons of the year the church will observe; this can happen even if your church doesn't closely follow the liturgical calendar. If choosing a thematic worship series, determine how long the series will last and its central theme.

   b. Brainstorm the major events and think critically about the rhythm of the congregation's year through worship. Think about what is necessary for this rhythm, what liturgical units will be included, and if there is any major space design that needs to happen through the season.

   c. Break the season/series into a weekly worship schedule. Once you have highlighted the full season/series, break it down into a manageable weekly worship schedule. At this point, depending on the size of your team, you can assign one or two people to lead each week's planning. This will allow for the labor of leading to be shared among the group, and for the diversity of the worship planning to be ensured through diverse leaders.

   d. Commence planning the weekly worship services for the season/series with the full worship planning team.

2. In planning weekly worship services:

   a. *Gather the group together in prayer.* Start the planning in prayer to center everyone's intention around God's work and will to be done in worship.

   b. *Hearing the Word Together.* Once you know the focus scripture(s) for the week's sermon, practice hearing the scripture read aloud multiple times (at least three). Each time the scripture is read, ask the following question from the group:

      1. What do you hear? Sounds? Particular words that resonate? Does a song come to mind?

2. What do you see when listening? Colors? Images?

3. What do you imagine happening in worship to prepare for this scripture? How would it be read? What happens before it is read? What might the scripture call for after the sermon?

c. *Imagining the Worship Flow.* After hearing the scripture and investigating the group's creativity sparked from the reading, begin to imagine the worship flow. How will the service move from a broad perspective? What will happen at the beginning, middle, and end? Many of the services will follow a standard worship flow; however, certain scriptures or liturgical seasons may offer room for a different flow. Be sure to take full care when imagining something different and include ways that you will liturgically introduce the congregation to the change.

d. *Creating the Worship Order.* This is where you will identify specific components of the worship service. Once the team agrees on the flow, you can begin to order the units and transitions of worship. Where will specific prayers happen? When will music happen? What will the congregation sing? All of the fine details get worked out in this time of planning.

e. *Recruiting the Worship Volunteers.* Don't forget to make use of the worship resource survey you have done to identify who is willing to offer their gifts to the community in worship.

f. *Thinking about Space.* Develop a vision for the space connected to either the theme of the season or week of worship. Once there is a general tone articulated, pass that information to the space planning small team and let them run with their creativity in bringing the vision to life. This part of the planning can happen earlier in the process as well.

g. *Communicating the Worship Plan.* Be sure to alert all persons involved of the plan for worship. This includes worship leaders, musicians, space design team, hospitality team members, and church staff members. If you are introducing something new to your congregation, it is helpful to also give them a heads up the week prior. This creates anticipation and keeps people from feeling completely caught off guard.

h. *Worship Together.* Now that all of the planning has been done, enter into worship knowing that God's Spirit will guide the service. We plan to create room for the Spirit's work to be manifested among the community.

i. *Reflecting.* Before you begin planning the next week of worship, spend some time reflecting on the service. Think about what happened. How was God's message carried through the entire service? How did the service reflect God's relationship with God's people, and the people's relationship with one another? How can this service inform the planning of the next few services?

The model proposed here does not ignore the challenges of collaborative worship planning. It requires great commitment and time, where many of us are already overscheduled.

While these challenges exist, it is important to prioritize planning worship together, and to maximize the time of the members of the planning team by creatively coordinating meeting schedules, using technology to facilitate many of those meetings, and dividing up responsibilities along the way. The main point to remember in the planning process is when church leaders co-labor they will find their services richer, more satisfying, and less frustrating.[5]

IDENTIFYING CONGREGATIONAL RESISTANCE TO WORSHIP

"Worship wars" are inevitable. They are as old as debates about the veneration of Jesus when he roamed first-century Palestine:

> But some were there who said to one another in anger, "Why was the ointment wasted in this way? For this ointment could have been sold for more than three hundred denarii, and the money given to the poor." And they scolded her. But Jesus said, "Let her alone; why do you trouble her? She has performed a good service for me. For you always have the poor with you, and you can show kindness to them whenever you wish; but you will not always have me. She has done what she could; she has anointed my body beforehand for its burial. Truly I tell you, wherever the good news is proclaimed in the whole world, what she has done will be told in remembrance of her." (Mark 14:4-9 NRSV)

How do we name what drives liturgical conflict? Is it preference or prejudice?

One of the overriding reasons for liturgical conflict comes out of what we already think liturgy or worship should be. Expressions or innovations that irk us likely do so not only because we disagree with the character of what they are but also because we have an idea of how things should be. Usually, how things should be liturgically rests upon what we already know and presume to constitute worship, rather than knowing what we might like or being open to how worship can stretch, challenge, and expand our liturgical sensibilities. For example, empirically, the majority of Christians in North America and the majority world privilege charismatic liturgical practice. Yet leaders of worship rarely associate glossolalia, the clapping of hands, collapsing, dancing, or shrieking in the spirit with liturgy.

What if we started instead from a place of liturgical openness and hospitality? In *The Worship Architect*, Constance M. Cherry suggests that hospitality makes "all the difference in the world" in the leadership of corporate worship. For her, the key to hospitable worship leadership is welcoming each guest into the liturgical assembly as if they were not only important, but necessary to worship.[1] How do we communicate the necessity of each worship participant, whether they inhabit the role of planner or participant? And how do we foster that atmosphere of openness (to new ideas and patterns of worship) in our congregation?

Cultivating this openness in our congregation and among our worship leaders molds and broadens the way we experience and reflect on worship. When reflecting on worship and ritual practice, we might ask the question whether worship worked. "Did the worship service do what the planning team or person thought it would?" "Was the liturgy effective?" "And what do we mean by 'effective?'" The ways to measure the impact of worship on participants to evaluate whether worship works are exponential. However, the bigger question is not a matter of efficacy—whether worship works. Rather, we should ask, How was the worship received and embodied by the congregation? And, What meaning did we make and what is the process of meaning-making that took place in worship? What did God reveal to us in worship? And, How did our worship connect not only to the word of God but also to the world of God, and all of the life within it? This moves us away from thinking about worship as a weekly pass or fail assignment, and instead toward a wider imagination and into a deeper engagement of how the worship service sets conditions for the gathered assembly to relate to God and one another.

In his book *Thinking Fast and Slow*, Daniel Kahneman offers a way for us to think about personal responses through what he calls *system 1* and *system 2* thinking. *System 1* thinking is a person's automatic and intuitive action to an experience. It is the initial response or way of responding to what someone witnesses or what is happening. It is the reaction that happens before recognition. *System 2* thinking kicks in when situations require more conscious and alert processing. It requires a person to slow down and pay greater attention to and think more critically about what they have experienced. This way of response is linked to learned behavior or time and can be seen in actions that are deemed second nature to us. *System 2* thinking moves beyond the impulsive responses in *system 1* and offers a more controlled and directed response that requires attention. We are not fully aware of these systems and how they operate in our lives. We spend much of our time operating in *system 1* as we go through our daily routines; however, *system 2* helps us dive more deeply.[2]

So, what does any of this have to do with worship and overcoming congregational resistance? In order to overcome congregational resistance, it is first key to imagine how certain liturgical actions prompt particular types of initial responses (*system 1*), and then how the fullness of the action moves the worship participants into deeper liturgical thought and engagement (*system 2*). In leading worship, part of the role is to help guide worshippers in learning how to think liturgically, and how to exercise control over their thoughts in liturgical moments. It is helping navigate the process of consciously deciding what does and does not have meaning in a given worship moment. In order to encounter resistance, worship leaders and participants are called to avoid remaining in our default system of thinking in worship, and to slow down in the liturgical practice to feel the depth of relation cultivated in the spiritual and personal community. Paying attention to our default patterns of response in liturgy can help us cultivate a fuller worship life.

Overcoming Congregational Resistance
Imagined through Systems Thinking

SYSTEM 1 WORSHIP RESPONSES	SYSTEM 2 WORSHIP RESPONSES
I am annoyed because someone is sitting in my seat.	That seat is taken today, I'll sit somewhere else and get a new angle in worship today.
I cringe at contemporary worship music.	This is not my style of music, but the meaning in the lyrics really speaks to my faith.
This prayer is too long.	Praying for matters of our world is important. God hears our prayers.
This kind of worship just doesn't do it for me.	Having an openness to experience styles and looking for the ways it reveals God in new and different ways is valuable.
Is God even here in this service?	How is God present in this service? How is God's presence manifested differently from what I am accustomed to in worship?
I did not like and don't agree with the sermon.	How does the sermon stretch my understanding of God? Why do I have some resistance to what I heard?
I don't know anyone there.	Making intentional steps to meeting new people in the congregation before or after worship can lead to personal growth.
I don't like the way the preacher is dressed. He is too casual. Her earrings are too distracting.	Creating an openness to what is being said over what I see, and moving beyond my own preferences and ideas of appropriate attire and appreciating what God is doing through the preacher is more important.

The crucial question of overcoming congregational resistance is focused on how people are shaped by worship. Is worship building the worshipper within his, her or their immediate (system 1) responses to liturgy? Is it challenging the worshipper by invoking deeper (system 2) thinking and practice in the liturgical moment? Does it connect to matters of the world and call us to engage those matters with worshipful thoughts and spirit?

Tools for Overcoming Congregational Resistance

- Keep the liturgical messaging simple.

- Create space for going deeper in worship (i.e., silence, prayer, worship talkbacks that engage the preacher's sermon content).

- Be aware of your own initial responses and what drives you to think more critically about liturgical actions.

137

- Be intentional in worship planning and leading.

- Give space for communal processing inside and outside of worship.

- Let the community speak (in action and in words) to what is relevant and holds meaning.

Questions and Exercises

1. Personal Reflection: What is your natural "default" setting in evaluating worship? Where do you find resistance? What are the areas in which you are most gracious and accepting? What preconceived ideas do you bring to worship? How do those ideas help or hinder your full engagement in worship?

2. How do you see system 1 and system 2 thinking at work in the liturgical life of your congregation? Can you imagine a way for these systems to operate in harmony?

3. Make a list of the common points of resistance you have witnessed among members of your congregation. Then list ways to overcome them. Think deeply about your proposed ways to overcome the resistances and visualize how to implement them worshipfully.

THE ARTS

In *Congregations in America*, sociologist of religion Mark Chaves (note that his last name rhymes with "waves") found that across churches, synagogues, mosques, and temples in the United States, three overlapping practices are primary: (1) worship, (2) the transmission of religious knowledge, and (3) celebration of the arts. They involve the most people, resources, and time within congregations. They also occupy more of congregational life than social service or political engagement.[1] Chaves admits that worship and religious knowledge transmission may not surprise many people as central congregational practices. But what about the arts?

By arts, Chaves does not distinguish between fine and popular, or "high" and "low."[2] Rather, he shows statistically that someone who attends worship will see visual art there more often than inside a museum, hear and make live music there more than within a concert hall, absorb and speak poetry, and experience and enact drama there more than within a theater (the dramatic exceeds what could be imagined sometimes!). In short, for Chaves, the arts give shape to worship, and worship incubates and celebrates the arts. His observation is a vital correction to the iconoclastic tendencies of historical Protestant reformers such as Thomas Müntzer, Andreas Karlstadt, Huldrych Zwingli, and Jean Calvin who likened iconography to idols. The research of Chaves even destabilizes modern iconoclastic stances such as ecclesiastical prohibitions against musical instrumentation in worship. Again, following the findings of Chaves, the very material content of any worship service is the arts. Chaves also sees the arts as empowering public witnesses of faith because the enthusiasm and investment in the arts of worship nurtures participation in worlds of art beyond the congregation.[3] This makes good sense as a tradition such as Methodism forged its theology from hymnody and gospel music became its own genre of popular art. More localized versions of the ability for the arts to provide a bridge from church to world may include a member of a congregation who chooses to sing in a community or school choir or the use of sacred repertoire in nonsectarian ensembles.

Importantly, for Chaves, worship and the arts are not synonymous practices. Not everything that happens in worship is best framed as art for him. Yet his claims suggest a further step in thinking about how generative it could be to think of the material content of worship as the arts. How would our overarching and particular vision for worship expand if we were to view every service as an artistic occasion? For example, homiletician Jacob D. Myers encourages leaders of worship to assume the role of curator, a role he sees as mysteriously tied to the Latin roots of *curare*, to "cure" and "care."[4] How might the varied artistic activities of worship be curated and assembled together in order to set conditions for encountering the healing and compassion of God and God's people as they practice mercy and doxology together?

Some services lend themselves naturally to artistic interpretation such as the Stations of the Cross or Youth Sunday. For others, designing and arranging the space, inclusive of liturgical paraments, furnishings, technology, and more, along with choreographing the poetry of prayer, proclamation, and testimony and weaving all of that into the musical, visual, and kinetic gifts of choir, instrumentalists, and congregationalists leads to imperfect seams or connections that may appear somewhat frayed or disjointed. Yet whether worship goes smoothly or feels as if it is a stretch or not quite put together, God shines light upon our quilted and patchwork efforts and in spite of them. We do not make worship holy, but we can lend a hand at expressing it in marveling ways.

It is also important to note that even as we advocate seeing worship as materially comprising the arts, we are not endorsing the use of worship as a spiritual talent show. If the material content of worship is already artistic, then there is no need to make it artsy. Rather, we recommend refining and beautifying what already exists for the glory of God as much as innovating new expressions to serve pastoral and congregational needs in the name of God. In that sense, even services that seem bare due to low attendance, limited or absent musicianship, or scarcity of other human or physical resources can become portals to the awe and wonder of Christ's love. For example, a simple sunrise prayer with two or three gathered together on Easter Sunday is a mystifying work of art.

Questions and Exercises

1. What happens when you identify and reinterpret the elements of your service as art? For example, how does the occasional service of a funeral change when we view it as dignifying mourning and providing a profound glimpse of hope in resurrected life?

2. Are you or others practicing artists? How might you resource your artistic gifts and the gifts of others not simply as contributions as discrete elements within a pattern of worship, but also to inspire new ways of thinking about the facilitation and offering of worship?

3. Art can operate like a commodity bought and sold like a stock. How does reframing worship as art provide an alternative way of valuing the aesthetic as a gift from God?

4. Artists push boundaries in their respective genres (dance, drama, film, literature, mixed media, painting, performance art, sculpture, and more) and in culture. What would it look like to push the boundaries of worship arts, not for the sake of novelty, but pastoral care? For example, could artistic thinking transform a Mother's Day service to help participants reconsider how to share Christian love to married and single mothers, mothers who have suffered losses such as miscarriage or the death of children, or women who long to be mothers but have not yet borne children or are unable to do so? Are there other "high holy days" where resourcing the arts might deepen the pastoral sensibilities of the service?

5. How might your church collaborate with artists? Think here of not only reaching out to "Christian artists." How might art become a bridge for connecting to the local community? And here, think liberally of artists. Perhaps a wedding planner could be invited for a non-matrimonial service to help with liturgical decor? Perhaps a chef could be invited to help prepare an after-service meal?

6. Suggestions for next steps in exploring the arts include the following:

> Invite your congregation to visit a museum, gallery exhibition, play, concert, comedy show, dance performance, or even a movie. See what ideas surface for strengthening the artistry of worship.

> Include in your pastoral library books that speak about the artistic process. Such titles are not simply coffee-table books with images. Rather, we are recommending artistic statements such as Ben Shahn's *The Shape of Content* (Harvard University Press, 1985), John Cage's *Composition in Retrospect* (Exact Change, 2008), Hito Steyerl's *Duty Free Art: Art in the Age of Planetary Civil War* (Verso, 2017), Chris Kraus's *Where Art Belongs* (Semiotexte, 2011), *The Artist Project: What Artists See When They Look at Art* (Phaidon, 2017), or Susan Leigh Foster's *Choreographing Empathy* (Routlege, 2011). If you don't feel like buying those titles, see if your church will give them to you. Or, ask your local library if it can procure them.

> Websites are also informative and provide easy access for liturgical ideas such as those of the Mississippi Museum of Art or Cleveland Museum of Art. There are also San Francisco's Exploratorium, New York's MOMA Ps1, Bentonville's Crystal Bridges of American Art, The City Museum of St. Louis, and more.

MUSIC

American poet Henry Wadsworth Longfellow is attributed as stating, "Music is the universal language of [hu]mankind." Of course we know from fields such as ethnomusicology that music comprises many different languages.[1] What one culture considers to be music, another might dismiss as noise, and that kind of musical exclusivism is problematic. Or, when we think of worship music, perhaps we first and almost always think of music in the English language even though the majority of God's people in the world do not speak English as their first language. Yet I (Khalia) remember hearing this Longfellow quote at a very early age. As I have gotten older, I have grown to understand it not as a presumed universality of music, but rather as witness to music's ability to reach the human soul in a unique and powerful way.

Music has potential to express and evoke the most basic human emotions where our own words may escape us. Philosopher Kathleen Marie Higgins describes it in her book *The Music Between Us* as music's ineffability, or its ability to "provoke experiences that exceed our linguistic capacity."[2] It is not that music genres are universally accepted, rather it is the idea of music's interior impact (even when manifested differently from one person to another) that is relatable across geography, language, race and ethnicity, social class, and human differences. Maybe another way to put it is that the universe is full of musical languages that move the human soul. We can only guess what kinds of music Jesus, the disciples, and the earliest house churches made for worship. Yet Edward Foley, in *Foundations of Christian Music*, suggests that it entailed an "intense lyricism," marked by responsive interactions peppered with "shouts, acclamation, hymns, improvised chants, and even the gift of tongues."[3] Here in the *Workbook*, we want you to think about music as a sonic unifier, even if it is not exactly universal.

Musical directors, concert musicians, and those tasked with either developing or organizing music order or playlists for public performance, or both, pay particular attention to song selections that create a vast connection for its audience. In similar ways, worship leaders have their own set of considerations when thinking about music for worship, including but not limited to selecting the proper music for the setting, how the music will function in the community, where it will be placed in the liturgy, and what music will speak to the cultural context of the church.[4] In worship, music plays a special role in the dialogue between God and God's people. It has the potential to shape the way we think and carry our proclaimed faith. Musical proclamation, particularly through lyrics, expresses the desires of God and our desires and actions for God.

Lyrical attention is key for balancing music that expresses something about God with music that responds to God's divine love and power, creating an opportunity for a shared communal declaration of God's majesty. The Psalter provides 150 chapters of biblical lyricism that easily lends itself to congregational song. Examples of worship songs that are expressions about the majesty of God include "How Great Thou Art," "A Mighty Fortress Is Our God," "Great Is Thy Faithfulness," "Heleluyan" [Muscogee/Creek Native American; "Alleluia"], "Siyahamba" [Zulu; "We Are Marching"], and "Inta Elaahi" [Arabic; "You Are My God"]. Songs that reflect God's action toward us, collectively as a congregation or inwardly with respect to personal piety, include "Amazing Grace"; "Guide Me, O Thou Great Jehovah"; and "I Want Jesus to Walk with Me." Songs in neighboring languages such as "Reoma Laboga" [Tswana; "We Give Our Thanks to God"], "La Ténèbre" [French; "Our Darkness"], "O So So" [Korean; "Come Now, Prince of Peace"], "Pui Si Vivimos" [Spanish; "If We Are Living"] also speak profoundly of God's devotion to us. It is helpful to know that there is a plethora of songs across "tongues of fire" that function in both ways. A healthy balance of both directional representations in our songs of worship—along with diversity in genre, sound, and language throughout the service—can afford multiple points of connection for the entire congregation, thus rendering a healthy and rich proclamation of the community's faith.

Instrumental music also shapes the mood and atmosphere of a worship service. We might readily associate the pipe organ, Hammond B-3 organ, piano, and acoustic and electric guitars with instruments typically found in a worship service. Perhaps strings, brass, and percussion ensembles or worship bands with folk, rock, and maybe even electronic music setups also make an appearance in worship services we have attended or led. Or maybe ethnic instruments beyond the djembe like taiko drums, singing bowls, mbiras, and erhus have resonated in services we have led or seen. You may want to push the frontiers of music making in worship by voicing the entanglement of our world still held and guided by the hands of God through experimentation with arhythmic, aleatory, melismatic, modal, and atonal lines and harmonies that do not follow a regular beat, intentionally appeal to sonic capriciousness, move in a more undulating and less predictable fashion, and outmaneuver typical key centers of Western music, even to the point of celebrating dissonance. Maybe you will decide to lead a choir where the organization of silence, breath, and tone say more than words. We encourage the use of all kinds of instrumentation, as well as musical technique and approach in worship to glorify God and to connect the people of God with one another and a God of musicalities without limits.

As you can see, worship music calls for careful consideration in worship planning. Whether the capabilities of your congregation are a full band or prerecorded music, whether you have mass choirs, small ensembles, or are pioneering other forms of worship musicality through sound design or that which we have not yet heard, thinking critically about music's function in your context will influence the overall tone of your service. What are the images of God presented in the lyrical content of the songs? How does the selected music connect with other parts of the service? In addition to closely considering the content of musical lyrics, does your music expand your understanding of God in terms of its register, key, tempo, rhythm, modality, and overall timbre? If a function of music in worship is the proclamation of our faith, expansive language and music style are key to wide inclusivity and praise in the name of God.

Exploring Different Music Styles for Worship

There are a number of music styles that add life to worshipping congregations. Provided below is a limited list that offers a summary of common music styles.

Historic Sacred Music—Dating back to the medieval era, traditional (or historic) sacred music has been an influential expression of European classical music. Most noted for impacting and inspiring the earliest written music (or notation), sacred music has shaped the way we sing. Sacred music, like Gregorian Chant, tends to hold a plainchant style that primarily holds one melody and has very little harmony.

Hymns—Written for the adoration and praise of God, hymns represent a very large and diverse genre of Christian music. The extensive history and development of hymns date back to antiquity, and have encountered extensive developments starting with the Protestant Reformation that brought two very different approaches to hymnody—one restricting hymns to only biblical-based content limiting what was sung and how; and another reformation approach that inspired a surge of hymn writing, production, and singing. Most hymns are written to a particular meter to allow for texts to be easily paired with hymn tunes for singing. Of the distinct variations of hymnody, African American hymns developed from spirituals brought about a very new anti-structured style of hymn singing, thus furthering the development Christian hymnody even more.

Gospel Music—Rooted in the Black oral tradition, the word *gospel* here speaks to a particular genre, as well as vocal and instrumental performance. This style, said to be pioneered by African American musician Thomas A. Dorsey, is marked by sound that is grounded in feelings, emotions, and personal religious experiences. Gospel vocal performance offers extensive vocal range and agility, and the musical instrumentation is a rhythmic compilation of blues, jazz, and popular music. Gospel has its own variation of sound including contemporary gospel and Southern gospel. The overall commonality in gospel music is the call for support of a choir congregation to carry out the singing, which is often led by a vocal worship leader.

Contemporary Worship Music—Often found in charismatic worship settings, contemporary worship music is characterized by songs led by a praise team or worship band, with one person—either the lead musician or singer—leading or directing the singing of the community. This genre is marked by repetition, melodies that are easy to learn, familiar chord progressions in order to be accessible for the entire community to sing, and lyrics that are more relational. Some churches and music groups that have popularized contemporary worship music are Hillsong, Bethel, and Elevation Church. For a more detailed account regarding "defining qualities" of contemporary worship music, see *Lovin' on Jesus* by Swee Hong Lim and Lester Ruth.[5] Of course, temporally speaking, French Taizé and Scottish Iona liturgical song might also be considered "contemporary."

Popular Music—In addition to the above styles of music, congregations may want to consider venturing beyond what is common to enhance their musical expressions of faith. Think about ways to include rock, Neo soul, hip-hop, jazz, pop music, and so much more into your repertoire. In 2018, Reverend Yolando Norton, assistant professor of Hebrew Bible and H. Eugene Farlough Professor of Black Church Studies at San Francisco Theological Seminary, introduced her Beyoncé Mass, which is a womanist worship service set to the pop artist's music and life experiences. Using popular songs that speak to lived experiences that African American women can relate to, Reverend Norton has transformed the way her target community sings of their relationship with God and their understanding of themselves as children of God. For some people, the Beyoncé Mass has revolutionized and magnified their praise to God and their engagement with biblical texts.

While the Beyoncé Mass is an extreme example, congregations can do something a bit simpler by taking small steps to move outside of the normal or comfortable ways of musicking and stretch to imagine more. For example, if the focus of the service is the Christian call to be light in a dark world, sing India.Arie's "I Am Light" and a communal proclamation and commitment to being divine light in this world. This is just one example, but with careful song selection and creative adaptation of lyrics, your congregation can tap into a wonderfully imaginative world of music that can offer different ways to proclaim your faith in God's divine love, justice, and community. One word of caution is to think critically about how (and if) you introduce popular music into your worship if it is not already a part of the ethos of your congregation. Also, popular music lyrics can tend to be written from the vantage point of personal experience with heavy use of "I" language. Be aware of the directional impact music will have in singing praise to God, and seek to strike a balance in how we are creating images of God's work in and through the community as we sing our faith together.

Sound Art and Sound Design—By sound art and sound design, we mean an open approach to crafting the musicality of any given service. In the West, sound art and sound design have roots as early as the nineteenth century with the use of the phonograph to create musical soundscapes, and within more focused exploration in avant-garde serious music of the Western classical tradition from the mid-twentieth century. Yet here, what we simply encourage is the use of vocal, instrumental, and electronic music in exploratory and experimental ways in order to evoke the sacred and expand the musicality producing the sense of the sacred in any given occasion of worship.

Questions and Exercises

1. Review your worship playlist. Think about the music offered in worship over the last three months. Even better, consider the entire repertoire of music offered in your worship services during a calendar year. Consulting previous printed orders of worship/bulletins, saved slides, and paid and volunteer musicians will help you assemble a catalog of worship music. Write down a full list of the instrumental pieces and songs and take time to review them carefully. What does the musicality of your particular context of worship say? How much of the material is repeated? How often, and how much does new music enter into your worship setting, and how is the new music embraced? Are diverse musical styles represented? Does the music offered in worship represent the full context and people of your congregation or place of worship? Is there room to imagine more in the sung and instrumental proclamation of your community's faith in God?

2. Popular music has long been an inspiration for reconfiguring Christian music, whether it is approximated with Christian Contemporary Music, Christian Hip-Hop, and so forth, or adopted directly in cover songs or rites such as a U2charist or Beyoncé Mass. Yet, how might overlooked genres or musical developments such as the free jazz compositional approaches of Bill Dixon or the sound design of Laurel Halo serve as influences for opening up the sonic palate of praise for any given assembly?

3. It is important that musical contributions are done "well." Yet does that mean that music in worship must be flawless? How might nonprofessional yet skilled musicians within your congregational context be encouraged and developed through musical practice and education as a part of the planning of worship?

4. It is also vital and theologically powerful to set a welcoming environment of worship music. What is the place of musical experimentation in worship? "Big ears" help open our consciousness to the expanse of music making possibilities for worship. Our communities of faith may already have a taste for other languages in congregational song and hymnody. But what about other melodies or arrangements of tones (even at the risk of sounding noisy) as a way of increasing participatory and audible awareness of how vast the presence and love of God is?

GOING SOLO

Much of this book takes into consideration the work of worship in a team environment, be it a large team or a small, three- or four-person team. But what about the solo pastors or worship leader volunteers who are single-handedly responsible for the planning and execution of weekly worship services? In these instances, there are limits to the worship leader's ability to bring the gifts and perspectives of all the people into the service. But you can make the best of what you have by leaning on the creativity and participation of your congregational volunteers. We want to offer two recommendations for the solo worship leader: (1) collaborate as much as it is possible, and (2) commit to self-care. In solo worship planning, there is often still an opening for partnership in planning, at least with one additional volunteer, usually a music leader.

Sometimes, collaborating with a musician will involve leaning on a rotation of willing song leaders and instrumentalists. We also suggest appealing to the congregation or assembly as a resource in all other aspects of worship leadership to help lighten the load and share the weight of driving the worship life for the congregation. Be creative as to how you use these resources. Perhaps you cast the vision, plan the services, and then invite members to lead different parts of the service during worship. Maybe you offer one service a quarter to be collectively planned with members of the congregation. There are different ways to rotate laity as partners in worship leadership without overtaxing them in terms of time and resources.

Maybe you are a bi-vocational worship leader. This brings in the complex factors of time, availability, and opportunity to collaborate with members of the congregation. It may feel like you are trying to be in two or three places at once.

If the 2020 global response to COVID-19 has taught us anything, it has expanded our personal capacity to imagine how to plan and lead worship virtually. Do not hesitate to use technology to connect with your volunteers to either plan worship or share information in preparation for worship leadership. If you are limited with laity who can lead within your congregation, look to create a worship leader working group. This can be a space where you and other solo or bi-vocational worship leaders come together quarterly, or as often as you determine, to think through the worship together. While you may not be leading the same services, these groups can help to inspire creative worship and offer different perspectives even when you may be the primary leader within your congregation. It is a way of sharing the heavy lifting of imagining more for your worship life. In addition, bring your bi-vocational life into the fullness of your worship leadership. Let it inform and motivate how you enter into your leadership. Maybe this means streamlining how, where, and how often worship happens. Who's to say that worship could not happen biweekly or once a month? Less can be theologically more! Look and listen for the ways God's direction, endurance, and comfort show up in the different spaces of your life to empower your worship efficiently as well as effectively. Treating porousness between your "sacred" and "secular" professional lives as an advantage and permitting yourself to rely upon grace from God and those you serve and love will keep you sane and spark creativity when conditions seem spartan and show (we pray) that you indeed have enough for faithful worship leadership.

Maybe you are responsible for multiple sites of worship. I (Gerald) began full-time ministry as a lead pastor serving four churches in Nottingham, England. It was difficult developing a vision for the congregations sharing my pastoral care because I did not see any one of them on a consistent, weekly basis in worship. In fact, one of the parishes was already struggling and eventually closed. Yet we managed to start the community's first Korean-language school in one sanctuary and resurrect a sunrise Easter service shared by all in a local nature reserve that was eventually broadcast on BBC radio. Our advice for multisite ministry as a solo pastor is to try and build a shared theological vision through printed and electronic materials that can be easily shared between volunteers (and any peers or colleagues) who may be supporting you. It may take some tinkering to find the best ways to get the word out and have it received, as well as develop adequate small group settings that feed into the primary worship service. Yet if a one-month, six-month, seasonal, or annual vision or theme (such as "unity in God" as it was underlying Gerald's earlier pastoral work) can be articulated and embedded within communications and opportunities for spiritual growth outside of the main service, we feel as if it can become an anchor that helps orient and unite multiple sites of ministry toward cohesive and shared theological growth even if worship services do not lend themselves to frequent spiritual nurturing from you.

As a solo worship leader, it is also important to consider matters of self-care. Don't try to do it all, even if it's all on you. Identify what you and your congregation do well and celebrate those talents. If fellow laity are not as available as you hope, do not hesitate to invite guests to help enliven your worship life and nurture its diversity of people. Finally, don't try to reinvent the wheel. Use the resources that are already available. Extraordinary worship does not have to be hard; it just needs to be thoughtful. It does not have to be novel; it just needs to be faithful, led by the Spirit of God and handled with great care. In that regard, solo worship leadership, like any type of worship leadership, seeks to love others as we love ourselves in the name of God. Just don't forget that you must first excel at loving yourself as a first step to leading extraordinary worship in your churches, especially if it seems like you're on your own.

Questions and Exercises

1. As a solo worship leader, create a list of worship gifts to distribute among your flock. Pass around the list during the offering. In the context of a worship service, explain that you are inviting volunteers to help you with worship planning. Give examples of what worship gifts might be: music making; writing and reciting prayers; reading scripture; baking Communion bread—heck, fermenting Communion wine—knitting paraments or providing other visual and sculptural art; decorating the altar; or providing flowers, candles, and so forth. Think also of where you would appreciate the most liturgical help.

Then make a direct invitation to others to help you in that area of need. For example, "Are there folks here who would be willing to give a testimony in church some time about how God has touched their lives?"

2. Make a list of colleagues (whom you know personally, or know of) who are solo worship leaders. Think about ways these individuals can come together as a group to support one another's work. Invite them into an initial conversation of forming an intentional working group and imagine how this group might take shape—a social media group exchanging innovations, challenges, and worship updates; or connecting through quarterly calls to reflect on worship from the previous quarter and thinking through worship for the upcoming quarter. Commit to connecting with this group, or with one or two persons on your list to build your network of like-minded conversation partners.

3. Revisit the last six months of worship you have led. What areas of the planning and leading process could have benefited from a rotation of volunteers? Who within your congregation could you have asked to share in the leadership? Think about how you can include these individuals in the worship planning and leading in the coming months.

RELEVANCE AS A CRUCIAL QUESTION

Asking about relevance is crucial for efficacious worship. Melva Costen writes that "in order for corporate worship to be authentic and empowering, it must be psychologically relevant to worshipers and commensurate with their lived experiences."[1] Inattention to questions of relevance risks liturgical narcissism. In a sense, every chapter of the *Workbook* has intended to help you focus upon a dimension of culture to make worship more relevant. One way to address relevance as a liturgical question is to begin by engaging the concept of liturgical inculturation. Peter C. Phan describes liturgical inculturation as "the double process of inserting the Gospel [*sic*] in a culture and the culture in the Gospel [*sic*] so that both are mutually enriched and challenged by each other."[2] Gospel and culture defy precise or absolute definition. They converge and diverge from each other in infinite ways. Gospel entails the justice, love, mercy, and grace of God revealed in the ministry and life of Jesus Christ and the gift of the Holy Spirit. Yet the gospel is also a product of culture.

The narratives of Jesus of Nazareth come from a particular time and a particular place and are influenced by the oral and written traditions of particular people throughout time. And those narratives are not only retold but also reworked in their transmission across time and place. It is important to recognize how the gospel is both shaping and shaped by culture. Then we begin to see how the Word of God always arises out of historical and political movement. This seems to be what Anscar Chupungco means when he describes inculturation as an incarnational imperative because from the incarnation we come to understand that Christ takes root in every culture.

At the same time, the gospel and its message of absolute love of God and neighbor challenge every culture and context. The gospel shines with a mercy that humankind cannot produce adequately or on its own. It is only that which God gives and empowers for sharing among every person in every place and epoch. To bring it closer to contexts of worship, Phan writes, the local church in its worship must become a "community of communities" and have at the center of its worship experience "dialogue."[3] Drawing upon shared wisdom from the Federation of Asian Bishops' Conferences of the Catholic churches in South, Southeast, East, and Central Asia, and especially in conversation with the work of Filipino Catholic liturgical reformer Anscar Chupungco, Phan specifies that careful liturgical inculturation commits to dialogue engaged in everyday life, political action with attention to liberation and justice, theological exchange between laity, clergy, and specialists, and the riches of religious experience across Christian and neighboring traditions.[4]

Liturgical inculturation must also entail acknowledging the cultural factors at work in defining what Christianity is and how we celebrate, challenge, and change it in Christian worship. To put it another way, relevance motivates the definitional, ecclesiastical, and social work of liturgical inculturation.

Culture encompasses the intervening complexities, interactivity, intimacy, and otherness shared between all planetary life (humans, plants, animals, macro- and microorganisms included) at home and abroad. As Phan writes, culture is a "historically evolving, fragmented, inconsistent, conflicted, constructed, ever-shifting, and porous reality."[5] Here, the definition of culture is purposely left open and unresolved because defining culture is politically contested by who has or assumes the authority and power to define what culture is as culture continually shifts and evolves. The liturgical line of interrogation we want to promote worship leaders to adopt with respect to liturgical inculturation has all kinds of practical dimensions.

One, for example, is to consider the differences in what we mean when we identify the eucharistic host or Communion wafer as the "bread of life," 生命的饼 [*Shēngmìng de bǐng*], and das Brot das Lebens. Are we actually imagining and partaking of the same thing within the contexts where English, Mandarin, and German are the lingua franca? In some ways, we are articulating unity and shared meaning in the Lord's Supper of the Christ. In other ways, the same sacramental gift is marked by vastly different languages and systems of social and cultural signification.[6] Put another way, liturgy that expresses belief and hope in a gospel shaping and shaped by culture should recognize how acquired theological knowledge and ritual action are always contingent upon who we are and where we are. And "who" and "where" are questions always up for grabs that for leaders of worship must be fundamentally asked with respect to a primary question of relevance informed by affirmations and objections regarding what we mean by gospel based upon historical inquiry, candid and trustworthy dialogue with an ever-growing exposure to neighbors, strangers, and enemies, learned, contested, and fashioned in political discourses, for the sake of making the love and mercy of God plain, accessible, and present in everyday life for everyday people.

Questions and Exercises

1. If the gospel shapes culture and is shaped by it, in what ways does your current leadership of worship form culture, and in what ways is your worship leadership informed by culture?

2. What aspects of culture do not figure in your planning and performance of worship? Why? As you identify cultural gaps in your worship leadership, which ones are worth filling? For example, if everyone shares the same political outlook in the assembly, what are ways to engage other points of view regarding what makes for a healthy society, especially in the name of God?

3. How does your worship respond "in real time" to major cultural shifts? What impact does the rapidly evolving social and political landscape have on your worship services? For example, how have seasons of social justice movements (protests, rallies, policy changes, etc.) shaped your worship, and how has your worship shaped either your congregation's engagement or perspective, or both, in these movements?

4. Using screen technology, references from popular culture, and self-disclosure are common devices used to make a worship service more relevant. How might a service become customized by observing and participating in the milieu of activity happening just outside of where your assembly meets? How would you go about it and for how long? With whom would you speak?

WHO ARE THE PEOPLE?

Leitourgia, or liturgy, is the work of the people. But who are the people to whom we have been referring during this entire book? If worship of God comes *from* the people who discern the desires and will of God through prayer, tradition, ritual, art, text, experience, reason, emotion, and more, and worship is *for* the people who accept the invitation to celebrate and practice the justice, peace, mercy, love, and grace given and called by God with one another and the rest of the world, we would be remiss to offer a resource for dynamic worship leadership without thinking about who the people of worship are. Worship loses integrity when we do not take the time to learn who our neighbors are. We liturgically ignore the second-most important teaching of Jesus: to love others as Christ has loved us.

Answering the "who" question may be straightforward in a general sense. The people are the people who gather inside sanctuaries, school gymnasiums and cafeterias, bars, outdoor parks and amphitheaters, concert and event venues, storefronts, warehouses, and all of the other various buildings that we inhabit and transform into temples of doxology for the divine. The people are the leaders and volunteers, lay and ordained, who make worship happen. Yet answering the "who" question becomes multifaceted when we take the time to ask questions such as, Who are we aiming to gather in worship? and What is going on in their lives that should figure into our worship-planning considerations? How do we find out what is happening in the lives who make up the work of the people that constitutes liturgy?

Barbara Holmes, in *Joy Unspeakable*, describes the church as a "living organism," ebbing and flowing with the "pulse of congregational life," reflecting "the local cultural and spiritual realities," and growing at the direction of the Holy Spirit.[1] As an organism, the church can grow, shrink, blossom, decay, live, and die. At the time of this writing, churches in the United States have been forced to close their doors to visitors even though they remain open in principle.

When churches were open, some congregations were so insistent that their forms of worship were most correct. In the classroom, we have sometimes witnessed this kind of liturgical snobbery when our students replace and become embarrassed about their free church roots for idealized notions of prayer book practices. When church as we know it is no longer possible as it was during the COVID-19 pandemic, this kind of hard-line liturgical thinking seems so far removed from what the situation demands—figuring out how to have worship at all when the conditions for it have completely changed. Whether or not a pandemic has struck, we think that the conditions for worship have already shifted dramatically and that they will continue to evolve in unexpected and drastic ways. What we recommend instead of an unrelenting adherence to liturgical formalism is a less rigid or, rather, more open commitment to form, and a more focused attention through prayer upon the needs of those who are worshipping, as well as the gifts that they bring to worship. By asking again and again who the people are, and how their collective work and gifts make worship come alive, we feel certain that you will develop a pastoral sensitivity dexterous enough to lead clearly in uncertain times and help your assembly remain sure-footed, but not heavy-handed in their efforts to produce robust and meaningful worship.

Questions and Exercises

1. Who are the people that make up the work of the people in your community of faith? Name them each by name. This might be relatively easy for a cozier gathering and challenging for a large ministry. Try to do it in any case, maybe not from memory, but as you look through your records of who attends worship. As you review the records, name these persons aloud and then pause and ask how much you know about their lives.

2. Do you know them in a detailed way or more casually? A little of both? Now, jot down a few notes to create a profile for each name that you named in exercise 1. Again, this may take less than an hour or be a project that requires a few days or more. In this case, the exercise here may be one that is done annually rather than on a regular basis. Keep at it. Once you have compiled a working file of the people in your community of faith, ask yourself how the dimensions of their lives inform what happens in worship. Does it? Or, do their lives mostly appear during moments of congregational prayer?

3. How might worship become more robust if it began with what is going on in the lives of those who are gathered as much or more than the denominational resources, manuals of prayer, hymnals and songbooks, web resources, and even scripture itself?

A CHANCE TO START CHURCH OVER

At the time of writing, a novel coronavirus, SARS-CoV-2 or COVID-19, is ravaging communities around the world. Gerald lives in New York and churches shut down midway through Lent. Khalia lives in Atlanta where most churches joined the rest of the country and closed their doors to physical in-person gatherings midway through Lent as well. Easter came and went without parishioners in pews. Pentecost too. And things still are not back to normal in Ordinary Time as we type. The churches are still open, in the sense that congregations are still worshipping, but they are having to enhance or improvise services on a screen or telephone. And some churches that chose to keep their doors open or reopened too soon have become incubators for viral infection, causing spikes in town and city-wide illness, and even death. Some parishioners have no worries about meeting in person. Others have become suspicious of any human encounter as a result of the pandemic. Our congregations and places of worship are being permanently altered by social distancing.

The greatest impact to worship during this 2020 global pandemic was the need for churches to quickly pivot to virtual worship, which for some congregations was a very new concept. Yet, broadcasting worship dates back to the advent of radio. The sermons of Clayton B. Wells appeared as early as the 1920s after Charles A. Stanley, president of the Cosradio Company and operator of amateur radio station 9BW in Wichita, Kansas, and a parishioner of Wells, was scolded by his pastor that if he was going to air on Sundays, he ought to have something about church. African American preachers like A. W. Nix, J. C. Burnett, J. M. Gates, and Pentecostals such as D. C. Rice and F. W. McGee soon followed on the airwaves, and gospel music provided African American artists a foothold in the growing technology even though they remained invisible.[1] So, the concept of opening up church by using technology to host worship is over a century old. Only now, social conditions are prohibiting the gathering of Christian worshippers in a way that differs from wartime or political oppression.

We have seen churches offer ingenious worship online. Some have had to scramble or amplify existing channels. Other congregations already possessed the infrastructure needed to telecast and graciously offered to help neighboring communities of faith go virtual. Whereas the newness of empty pews may have been a major disruption for all, in some modern congregations, it was already old hat for the pastor, liturgists, and musicians to appear from afar and onscreen. We believe that digital worship is only the beginning of new expressions to come. One upside to the havoc wreaked by COVID-19 is that it pushed us into the twenty-first century. Now that we have experimented liturgically within the new era, we believe that some and perhaps many of the changes are here to stay. God forbid that another pandemic or other social catastrophe forces our liturgically innovative hand. As we move forward from COVID-19, we recommend that leaders of worship retain or nurture the kind of agility that made worship possible when sanctuaries across the world were closed.

Maybe Communion on the World Wide Web is not that bad. Perhaps it provides another way of attending to "presence in the absence." John Wesley fretted over ordaining clergy outside of the Church of England so that they could offer sacraments to the churches of the budding Methodist movement. Who is to say that the closure of sanctuaries is not also as good of a reason as the growth of a spiritual movement to rethink what is appropriate and liturgically responsible in terms of offering the body and blood of Christ? Though she focuses upon how to act within a declining church, and is not addressing a literally empty sanctuary building, Shannon Craigo-Snell in *The Empty Church* provides a thought-provoking claim: "Church must remain empty in response to the grace of God and in recognition that grace comes from God alone and not from human efforts. Both divine revelation and human faith are gifts of God."[2] Whether we are streaming services or using digital technology to reimagine worship and forge new liturgical ground, the prospect and reality of empty sanctuaries could operate like a womb in which new liturgical expressions are nurtured and born.

For the younger generations, this shift to enhanced use of technology was quite familiar, while for older generations it took time to learn and adjust. In some congregations, there became an immediate intergenerational connection as younger members of worshipping communities worked to help get older members connected to their virtual worship. These changes have caused churches to interact in a new way and reimagine what it means to be community. It has all called for a reimagination of worship that is more inclusive. Many churches have seen greater numbers of participation in online worship due to greater access. For example, churches reported an increase in attendance for their online midweek Bible studies with more of their senior members attending. This is a result of these members having an option to join from home rather than having to risk driving to the physical building in the evenings, which many choose not to do. Other churches have found more engagement from youth and young adults in Sunday school classes by shifting the times of the virtual gatherings to early afternoons or to another day of the week. How might the witness of these types of examples impact the future of your congregation's communal engagement? What are the points of change that might be sustained to cultivate greater access and interest for your members?

Many lessons have been learned and shared along the way through COVID-19. Churches have become more collaborative in imagining their new ways of being and are sharing best practices, mistakes, and ideas much more readily than before. Many pastors and worship leaders around the country formed working groups to share virtual creative space as they tried to live into an imposed reality. Webinars, live streams, and carefully curated panels brought together diverse groups of thought leaders—practitioners to attend to matters of health, safety, and the digital church. Music leaders have experimented and collaborated in ways that have sparked new ideas and energy in music teams. The measure of care and creativity that was shared in a time of global trauma witnesses an amazing measure of hope to be found in the collective unity of the body of Christ. However, at the same time that some churches found their rhythm and stride in the digital worship world, it is important to recognize that many congregations did not. Some churches had to close their doors permanently due to lack of resources. Other churches felt the pressure to reopen as early as possible for a myriad of reasons. And many pastors are witnessing the reality of digital worship burnout. As we live in the tension of these realities, there are many lessons to be learned to inform and shape how we exist as worshipping congregations beyond COVID-19.

During this time, we engaged in many conversations with pastors and worship leaders for the sake of our own work and to inform the writing of this book. The feedback given was insightful, eye opening, and prompted great food for thought in imagining the future of worship. Below is a short summary list of key ideas and best practices that resonated across different cultural and ecclesial congregations and offer foundational points to ponder for the future of congregational worship.

Conversations with Pastors and Worship Leaders

- Shortening worship services for digital engagement was necessary. Services were frequently trimmed to thirty to forty-five minutes to account for viewer attention spans. For some congregations, this required eliminating a lot of the worship elements that were ingrained in the worship community, and to reimagine what parts of the service were most important to keep.

- Less is more. Doing less creates a more impactful experience in digital worship. Keeping worship simple yet creative is a consistent theme.

- Increase your digital engagement beyond the weekly service. Make use of the digital platforms to communicate with your virtual congregation through social media posts, email contact, and so on. Offer an encouraging word through a one-minute video message, or a text-based thought. Send highlights from the previous service as a point of connection through the week.

- Involve the community members. The move to digital worship for some churches meant the pastor and a select few worship leaders were the primary participants in leading worship. However, some congregations found it important to involve the community in different ways (i.e., reading scripture, sharing their journey through testimony, etc.).

- Be intentional about diversity. It is very easy to lose sight of maintaining diversity when in the rhythm of producing digital worship, particularly services that have fewer components. Maintaining this focus on the front end of the planning was crucially important. Representation matters just as much, and maybe more, in digital worship.

- Think beyond the congregation who shows up in the building every Sunday. Moving to digital worship expands your reach and broadens your audience base. How are you connecting with first-time viewers? What steps are you taking to make viewers feel engaged and connected to the service?

- Think creatively about the use of digital platforms. If using Zoom for worship, offer small group discussions following the service for people to reflect on worship. Use quotes from the sermon to prompt discussion.

- On all platforms that offer a chat feature, invite volunteers to serve as engagement hosts to maintain and encourage interaction during the service. Assign different roles to each volunteer—have someone manage the standard hospitality and informational communication and have someone else engage any new visitors and the ongoing chat discussion generated by the service.

- Be aware of the pros and cons of prerecorded service versus live services. Both provide different advantages. Prerecorded services allow for the ability to incorporate more members into the experience through their own video recordings. They also give more opportunity to add variety in the service through different imagery through the service, different points of view with camera angles, and lets you work a few weeks ahead. However, prerecorded services require dedicated editing, and some congregations do not have the resources. Live online services allow for a more "in the moment" experience, and do not require any postproduction.

What is shared above is a summary of thoughts from a collective group of worship leaders. I am sure you have found experiences that can be added to this list. Consider these points as part of a larger and ongoing conversation around the globe on how we are to worship. We have learned a lot in the face of a global pandemic. Our prayer is that we all take a moment to see what God is doing in the inbreaking of our chaos.

Questions and Exercises

1. Reflect on the changes your congregation made as a result of COVID-19. What worked? What didn't work? Why? What have these changes taught you about the way you were worshipping before? What did they teach you about your community's worship identity? What have you found to be most important to your worship context in these times? How can this discovery inform your future worship?

2. How might you sustain the digital worship that you have engaged? What needs to be improved? What might you do differently? What do you need to maintain a consistent digital worship presence? What resources do you already have and how are you using them? In what ways can a digital worship component continually reinvigorate your worship creativity?

3. The most frequent point shared from congregations was the members' desire to feel connected to their community from whom they had been abruptly separated during COVID-19. In the absence of sheltering in place, are there members of your community who carry this same sentiment because of the inability to be in community at the church due to illness, inability to commute, and so forth? How might you continue virtual practices of community to ensure this segment of your worship is included?

4. Beyond the worship service engagement, what are creative ways to continue to connect with your congregation virtually through the week? If you do not have full digital capacity to livestream or hold video conferences, how can you use an audio conference call or email to motivate your congregation in worshipful ways? Being creative does not have to mean inventing something outside of your reach. However, it does require consistency.

5. How can you build digital worship into the future of your congregation as a matter of self-care and energy conservation? For solo pastors, what might it look like to build a rhythm of online worship into your year to give spaces for you, the congregation, and even your facility to breathe and rest? For example, you may choose to worship virtually during the month of July as a way of staying engaged while encouraging a time of rejuvenation. Perhaps you even build a series of worship around rest during this time. Or build in a week of digital worship every quarter.

HOW THEN SHALL WE GATHER? PASTOR REFLECTIONS ON VIRTUAL WORSHIP

Chris Jorgensen, pastor at Hanscom Park United Methodist Church in Omaha, Nebraska

Pastors make all kinds of judgments about how to worship every week. Shall we follow the liturgical calendar? How often should we celebrate Communion? Robe or no robe? Which words do I use in prayer and in preaching? The list goes on and on. However, I never asked whether the gathering of human bodies is a requirement of worship until such gathering was made impossible. When I found myself in the midst of a global pandemic in March 2020, when physical gathering was unsafe, I wondered for the first time, In order to worship, must people gather together? In other words, is virtual worship *actually* worship?

I was trained to answer in the negative. My worship textbook from seminary was very clear on this point. According to James F. White, physical gathering is absolutely essential when we worship. White identifies the act of gathering as the difference between "personal devotions" and "common worship." He writes that "the clearest aspect of common worship is that it is the worship offered by the gathered congregation, the Christian assembly."[1]

My Methodist tradition seems to concur. The founder of the Methodist movement, John Wesley, encourages the engagement of what he called the "means of grace." Wesley includes acts of personal and communal piety (prayer, worship, studying scripture alone and in community, receiving Communion) and mercy (visiting the sick, giving to the poor, visiting the prisoner) as means or conduits of God's grace. These means all function toward one end: "bringing a sinner to salvation." Wesley differentiates between personal prayer and praying with "the faithful" in "the great congregation."[2]

Does that mean that when we do not or cannot gather in person with one another, we cease to worship? Is what one might call virtual worship in fact a time of personal devotion: a work of piety between oneself and God, simply mediated by a set of digital sounds and images? The answer is in the question of gathering. Social media platforms such as Facebook, YouTube, and Zoom (and certainly many others undoubtedly springing up between the moment of this writing and your reading) offer the necessary technology not just to watch or observe worship but to *gather* virtually for worship.

Synchronously or asynchronously, these platforms allow for interactive communal experiences of worship through the participation of the gathered community. Smaller congregations gather through Zoom so that each person is able to see and hear the "great congregation" engaged in worship at the same moment. Facebook Live offers the opportunity for people in physically remote places to greet one another, share prayer requests, and offer responses to the sermon via textual comments. One could argue that this makes worship even *more* communal than when worshippers are sitting but perhaps disengaged in the pews. As these technologies and pastoral familiarity with them develop, ever-more robust opportunities for virtual gathering will arise.

Gathering in worship is critically important to the Christian life. We worship and employ all of the means of grace, as noted by Wesley, to "bring the sinner to salvation." For Wesley, this salvation was both an event and a process. In my preferred vernacular, we worship in order to enable a transformative encounter with God in Christ, and then regular worship enables a lifetime of such transformation and growth into the image of God. As John Calvin said, "We are lifted up even to God by the exercises of religion. What is the design of the preaching of the Word, the sacraments, the holy assemblies, and the whole external government of the church, but that we may be united (conjugant) to God."[3] Practiced with integrity and intention, virtual worship can be that holy assembly that enables salvation through human unity with the divine.

Questions and Exercises

1. In two sentences, write down your understanding of the purpose of worship. What challenges does virtual worship pose given your own definition? How would you overcome the challenges identified?

2. White insists that gathering is the most fundamental aspect of Christian worship; however, when we worship together virtually, this gathering happens without the proximity of physical bodies. How might worship leaders evoke a sense of gathering in the virtual world? Design an activity or ritual to be employed as part of a virtual worship service that enhances the virtual community's sense of being a "gathered" people.

3. Rewrite a prayer, liturgy, or sermon that you have used in traditional corporate worship in order to make it more effective in a virtual worship setting.

4. Research either your denomination's or judicatory's position on celebrating virtual Eucharist/Communion. What are the practical and theological challenges to virtual Communion? What are the practical and theological benefits to offering virtual Communion? If allowed, to what requirements must virtual communion celebrations adhere? Why?

5. Adapt a eucharistic prayer from your tradition to account for the spatial distance of participants and variability of elements employed by people in their home worship settings.

REVELATION

Revelation 7:9-10 has inspired the entire book:

After this I looked, and there was a great crowd that no one could number. They were from every nation, tribe, people, and language. They were standing before the throne and before the Lamb. They wore white robes and held palm branches in their hands. They cried out with a loud voice:

> "Victory belongs to our God
> who sits on the throne,
> and to the Lamb."

No one exactly knows what Revelation means here. Yet we do get an idea of God's desires for Christian worship. God wants a countless and all-encompassing gathering of people from every place praising the Lamb. It may seem like fantasy. But we can apprehend here a shared universal *telos* for Christian worship—summoning the Imago Dei of the world into totalizing doxology.

God is calling leaders of Christian worship to inspire and invite all people, creatures, and things into the glory of God. Today, it may look like diversifying our congregations or finding a way to boost attendance and participation in person or online. Or, it may mean something measurable and miraculous. However it takes shape, we want to suggest that every occasion of worship ought to provide a glimpse of people from every nation, and all tribes, peoples, and languages praising the Lamb of God. Without a preview of God's future now, Christianity separates itself from the reality and truth of the gospel. It amounts to scriptural lore.

The exercises in this book have aimed to empower wider ways of liturgical welcome. They have promoted liturgical flexibility for the sake of increasing accessibility to the gospel of Christ. Everything has not been covered. We did not, for example, devote a section to prayer, which might seem like an elemental oversight.[1] Yet prayer has inspired every page. Every discussion, question, and exercise above are prayers intended to awaken a particular kind of attention to generally underappreciated aspects of worship in order to ignite practices that help the eschatological horizon of Revelation come into focus. We give God thanks for your time and for you in working through what we have offered.

NOTES

Introduction: The Work of the People

1. Thomas H. Troeger and Leonora Tubbs Tisdale, *A Sermon Workbook: Exercises in the Art and Craft of Preaching* (Nashville: Abingdon Press, 2013), 1.

2. Giorgio Agamben, *The Omnibus Homo Sacer* (Palo Alto, CA: Stanford University Press, 2017), 956.

3. Karl Ove Knausgaard, *My Struggle: Book I* (New York: Farrar, Straus and Giroux, 2009), 267.

4. Karl Barth, "The Election of the Individual: The Determination of the Rejected," in *Church Dogmatics, II/2*: 498–563. Edinburg: T & T Clark, 1957.

2. The Mystery of Our Jewish Roots

1. John G. Gager, *Who Made Early Christianity? The Jewish Lives of the Apostle Paul* (New York: Columbia University Press, 2015), 3.

2. Carolyn Osiek and Margaret Y. MacDonald, with Janet H. Tulloch, *A Woman's Place: House Churches in Earliest Christianity* (Minneapolis: Fortress, 2005).

3. For more on the Jewishness of the New Testament, especially with respect to the Apostle Paul, see Gager, *Who Made Early Christianity?*

4. John Chrysostom, *Discourses against Judaizing Christians*, 1.3.1 (Washington, DC: Catholic University Press, 1979), 11. With thanks for the initial reference to Catherine Nixey, *The Darkening Age: The Christian Destruction of the Classical World* (London: Macmillan, 2017), 133.

5. Nixey, *The Darkening Age*, 133.

6. Lauren Winner, *The Dangers of Christian Practice: On Wayward Gifts, Characteristic Damage, and Sin* (New Haven, CT: Yale University Press, 2018), 49.

7. Julie Zauzmer, "The Alleged Synagogue Shooter was a Churchgoer Who Talked Christian Theology, Raising Tough Questions for Evangelical Pastors," *Washington Post*, May 1, 2019, https://www.washingtonpost.com /religion/2019/05/01/alleged-synagogue-shooter-was-churchgoer-who-articulated-christian-theology-prompting -tough-questions-evangelical-pastors/.

8. *Oxford English Dictionary*, s.v. "supersessionism," Oxford University Press, 2020, available at Lexico.com, accessed November 19, 2020.

3. Liturgical Time

1. Robert Knapp, *The Dawn of Christianity: People and Gods in a Time of Magic and Miracles* (Cambridge, MA: Harvard University Press, 2017), 3.

2. Alden A. Mosshammer, *The Easter Computus and the Origins of the Christian Era* (New York: Oxford University Press, 2008), 8.

4. Tradition

1. Maxwell E. Johnson, "Imagining Early Christian Liturgy: The *Traditio Apostolica*—A Case Study." In *Liturgy's Imagined Past/s: Methodologies and Materials in the Writing of Liturgical History Today*, ed. Teresa Berger and Bryan D. Spinks (Collegeville, MN: Liturgical Press, 2016), 100.

2. Robert Taft, "The Structural Analysis of Liturgical Units: An Essay in Methodology," in his *Beyond East and West: Problems in Liturgical Understanding* (Washington, DC: Pastoral Press, 1984), 153–54.

3. Maxwell E. Johnson, "The Apostolic Tradition," in *The Oxford History of Christian Worship*, ed. Geoffrey Wainwright and Karen B. Westerfield Tucker (New York: Oxford University Press, 2006), 38.

4. Paul Bradshaw, *Early Christian Worship: A Basic Introduction to Ideas and Practice* (Collegeville, MN: Liturgical, 2010), 17.

5. Bradshaw, *Early Christian Worship*, 45–46.

5. The Inscrutable Preference for Two Patterns

1. For a more nuanced and historical discussion of the defining qualities of contemporary worship, see Swee Hong Lim and Lester Ruth, *Lovin' on Jesus: A Concise History of Contemporary Worship* (Nashville: Abingdon, 2017), 2–3. Also note that the effusive liturgical traditions described here have a long tradition in the history of US revivalism. See also Francis Fitzgerald, *The Evangelicals: The Struggle to Shape America* (New York: Simon & Schuster, 2017), 21. Even the history of Princeton Theological Seminary is tied to extreme worship reactions from the nineteenth century.

Though he focuses primarily upon the musical dimensions of modern Christian worship, in Gerardo Marti, *Worship across the Racial Divide: Religious Music and the Multiracial Congregation* (New York: Oxford University Press, 2012), 116–17, Marti describes a tripartite pattern of worship as the "ideal-typical worship pattern" that moves from orientation to meditation to celebration.

For ideas regarding how to invigorate existing mainline Protestant patterns with the goods of contemporary worship, see Lester Ruth, ed., *Flow: The Ancient Way to Do Contemporary Worship* (Nashville: Abingdon, 2020).

2. Gordon Lathrop, *Holy Things: A Liturgical Theology* (Minneapolis: Fortress, 1998), 19, 54. Lathrop writes that "the liturgical pattern is drawn from the Bible" and that "the experiences of both faith and scripture, both faith and meal prayers, both faith and week, simply became new worship patterns." See also, Martha Moore-Keish, "The Importance of Worship that Centers on the Ordo," *Liturgy* 21, no. 2 (May 2006): 15–23.

3. Valeriy A. Alikin, *The Earliest History of the Christian Gathering: Origin, Development, and Content of the Christian Gathering in the First to Third Centuries* (Leiden: Brill, 2010).

4. See M. Klinghardt, *Gemeinschaftsmahl und Mahlgemeinschaft. Soziologie und Liturgie frühchristlicher Mahlfeiern* (Tübingen/Basel: Francke, 1996); H. J. de Jonge, "The Early History of the Lord's Supper," in *Religious Identity and the Invention of Tradition*, ed. J. W. van Henten and A. Houtepen (Assen: Van Gorcum, 2001), 209–37; and Dennis Smith, *From Symposium to Eucharist: The Banquet in the Early Christian World* (Minneapolis: Fortress, 2003).

5. Alikin, *The Earliest History of the Christian Gathering*, 20.

6. Alikin, *The Earliest History of the Christian Gathering*, 20–23.

7. Rowan Williams, "Naming the World: Liturgy and the Transformation of Time and Matter," in *Full of Your Glory: Liturgy, Cosmos, Creation*, ed. Teresa Berger (Collegeville, MN: Liturgical Press, 2018), 33.

6. Scripture

1. Johnson, "The Apostolic Tradition," in *The Oxford History of Christian Worship*, 36–37.

2. Johnson, "The Apostolic Tradition," 45–48. Johnson mentions as possible sources for the table prayers of Jesus and the disciples the Greco-Roman *symposion*, *convivium* ("the post-meal 'drinking party'"), lost oral traditions, and Bryan Spinks discrediting the assumption that standardized Jewish prayers such as the *birkat ha-mazon* would have been preferable without documentary evidence given the availability of other meal prayers.

7. Other Sacred Texts

1. Mark Smith, "'What Have Canaan and Babyl to do with Israel?' The Problem of Ancient Near Eastern Divinity in the Biblical Godhead," Helena Professor of Old Testament Literature and Exegesis inaugural lecture, February 11, 2020, Princeton Theological Seminary.

2. "The African American Lectionary: A Collaborative Project of The African American Pulpit and American Baptist College of Nashville," http://www.theafricanamericanlectionary.org/about.asp, accessed May 11, 2020.

8. Interreligious Dialogue

1. Shira Schoenberg, "Ashkenazism," Jewish Virtual Library, https://www.jewishvirtuallibrary.org/ashkenazim, accessed May 11, 2020.

2. Rebecca Weiner, "Sephardim," Jewish Virtual Library, https://www.jewishvirtuallibrary.org/sephardim, accessed May 11, 2020.

3. "Sunnis and Shia: Islam's Ancient Schism," BBC News, January 4, 2016, https://www.bbc.com/news/world-middle-east-16047709, accessed May 11, 2020.

4. "Sunnis and Shia: Islam's Ancient Schism."

5. Kathleen (Kathy) Black, with Bishop Kyrillos, Jonathan L. Friedmann and Tamar Frankiel Hamid Mavani and Jihad Turk, *Rhythms of Religious Ritual: The Yearly Cycles of Jews, Christians, and Muslims* (Claremont, CA: Claremont Press 2018), 3.

9. The Sacraments—Baptism

1. Bradshaw, *Early Christian Worship*, 4.

2. Bradshaw, *Early Christian Worship*, 4.

3. Rowan Williams, *Being Christian: Baptism, Bible, Eucharist, and Prayer* (Grand Rapids, MI: Eerdmans, 2014), 10.

10. The Sacraments—Eucharist

1. Paul F. Bradshaw, *Reconstructing Early Christian Worship* (Collegeville, MN: Pueblo, 2009), 10.

2. Bradshaw, *Reconstructing Early Christian Worship*, 4–5.

3. Bradshaw, *Reconstructing Early Christian Worship*, 5.

4. At the time of this writing, online Communion has become a regular feature of worship as churches adjusted their table practices to observe state and federal regulations in response to the COVID-19 pandemic.

5. Teresa Berger, *@Worship: Liturgical Practices in Digital Worlds* (New York: Routledge, 2018), 25.

6. Ruth Ann Daily, "Church Should Weather Harsh Words," *Pittsburgh Post-Gazette*, May 29, 2002.

7. Gerald C. Liu, "Christmas Eve Communion: A Story of Sacramental Recovery," *Worship Arts*, November–December 2015, 7–9.

11. Preaching

1. Troeger and Tubbs Tisdale, *A Sermon Workbook*.

2. Alistair Stewart-Sykes, *From Prophecy to Preaching: A Search for the Origins of Christian Homily* (Leiden: Brill, 2001).

3. Thomas H. Troeger, *The End of Preaching* (Nashville: Abingdon, 2018).

4. Troeger, *The End of Preaching*, 10.

5. Troeger and Tubbs Tisdale, *A Sermon Workbook*, 116–17.

6. See a formalized version of Ted Smith's method here: "How to Preach without Notes," https://www.sermoncentral.com/pastors-preaching-articles/ted-smith-how-to-preach-without-notes-1531, accessed June 8, 2020.

12. Languages of Liturgy and Worship

1. Louis-Marie Chauvet, "Are the Words of the Liturgy Worn Out? What Diagnosis? What Pastoral Approach?" paper presented at the North American Academy of Liturgy Annual Meeting, Baltimore, Maryland, January 4, 2009.

2. Geoffrey Wainwright, *Doxology: The Praise of God in Worship, Doctrine, and Life* (New York: Oxford University Press, 1980), 18.

3. Janet R. Walton, *Feminist Liturgy: A Matter of Justice* (Collegeville, MN: Liturgical Press, 2000), 28.

4. Walton, *Feminist Liturgy*, 31.

13. Weddings

1. "The Knot 2019 Real Weddings Study," The Knot, https://www.wedinsights.com/report/the-knot-real-weddings, accessed April 22, 2020. Most of our discussion and its suggestions respond to The Knot study.

2. These events actually happened in a wedding attended by one of the authors in the summer of 2019.

3. "Introduction: The Christianization of Marriage," in *How Christian Marriage Became One of the Sacraments: The Sacramental Theology of Marriage from Its Medieval Origins to the Council of Trent* by Philip L. Reynolds (Cambridge: Cambridge University Press, 2016), xiii–xxx.

4. Willie James Jennings, *Acts: A Theological Commentary on the Bible* (Louisville: Westminster John Knox, 2017), 60.

5. Jennings, *Acts*, 60.

14. Funerals

1. Thomas G. Long, *Accompany Them with Singing: The Christian Funeral* (Louisville: Westminster John Knox, 1994).

15. Other Occasional Services

1. Susan Bigelow Reynolds, "From the Site of the Empty Tomb: Approaching the Hidden Grief of Prenatal Loss," *New Theology Review* 28, no. 2 (March 2016): 59. The actual quotation from Bigelow contains what seems to be a typo, "of his dear friend, a women [*sic*] bewildered by grief." We have changed it above based upon John 20:15-18.

See also, United States Conference of Catholic Bishops, "Blessing of Parents after a Miscarriage or Stillbirth," last accessed May 27, 2020. http://www.usccb.org/prayer-and-worship/bereavement-and-funerals/blessing-of-parents-after-a-miscarriage-or-stillbirth.cfm.

2. Our thanks to the Reverend Dr. Christy Bonner for informing us of National Pregnancy and Infant Loss Remembrance Day.

16. Sacred Space

1. Heather Murray Elkins, review of *Worship Space Acoustics: 3 Decades of Design*, edited by David T. Bradley, Erica E. Ryherd, and Lauren M. Ronsse. *Homiletic* 42:1.

2. Jeanne Halgren Kilde, *Sacred Power, Sacred Space: An Introduction to Christian Architecture and Worship* (New York: Oxford University Press, 2008), 4.

3. Jonathan Z. Smith, *To Take Place: Toward Theory in Ritual* (Chicago and London: The University of Chicago Press, 1987).

4. Kilde, *Sacred Power, Sacred Space*, 7.

5. James F. White and Susan J. White, *Church Architecture: Building and Renovating for Christian Worship* (Akron, OH: OSL Publications, 2002).

6. White and White, *Church Architecture*, 123. See also pages 122–25. Moreover, we recommend that readers who are especially interested in details regarding how to organize and build sacred space read the entirety of White and White.

7. White and White, *Church Architecture*, 111.

8. https://www.creationjustice.org/mission.html, accessed June 18, 2020. For resources on practical steps toward an eco-justice– focused worship service, see http://www.creationjustice.org/uploads/2/5/4/6/25465131/sacred _spaces.pdf.

9. Howard Thurman, *The Inward Journey* (Richmond, IN: Friends United, 1961), 112.

10. Thurman, *The Inward Journey*, 112.

17. Ecology and Worship

1. Author's note: I capitalize the word *Creation* throughout this essay to denote the level of respect afforded the other-than-human world as subject rather than object. I do the same with the word *Earth* when addressing it as an entity (as opposed to lowercase *earth*, a synonym of soil).

2. According to a 2014 study, Americans who say their clergy leader speaks at least occasionally about climate change are more likely to believe it exists than Americans who tend not to hear about climate change in church (49 percent and 36 percent, respectively). More than six-in-ten Americans who report hearing about climate change from their clergy leader at least occasionally are very (38 percent) or somewhat (24 percent) concerned about climate change. See Robert P. Jones, Daniel Cox, and Juhem Navarro-Rivera, *Believers, Sympathizers, and Skeptics: Why Americans Are Conflicted about Climate Change, Environmental Policy, and Science: Findings from the PRRI/AAR Religion, Values, and Climate Change Survey* (Washington, DC: Public Religion Research Institute and American Academy of Religion, 2014), 4.

3. See also Ruth Duck, *Worship for the Whole People of God: Vital Worship for the 21st Century* (Louisville: Westminster John Knox, 2013), 3.

4. Benjamin Stewart, *A Watered Garden: Christian Worship and Earth's Ecology* (Minneapolis: Augsburg Fortress, 2011), 11.

5. Ferris Jabr, "How Humanity Unleashed a Flood of New Diseases," *New York Times*, June 17, 2020, https://www.nytimes.com/2020/06/17/magazine/animal-disease-COVID.html?action=click&auth=login -email&login=email&module=Editors%20Picks&pgtype=Homepage, accessed June 22, 2020.

6. Leah D. Schade, *For the Beauty of the Earth: A Lenten Devotional* (St. Louis: Chalice, 2019), 1.

7. Matthew Sleeth, *Reforesting Faith: What Trees Teach Us about the Nature of God and His Love for Us* (New York: Waterbrook, 2019).

8. According to the California Department of Forestry and Fire Protection, in 2017 alone, wildfire firefighting agencies responded to 9,270 fires that burned 1,548,429 acres, many of them in vineyard country. See California Department of Forestry and Fire Protection, "2017 Wildfire Activity Statistics," https://www.fire.ca.gov /media/10059/2017_redbook_final.pdf, April 1, 2019, accessed June 20, 2020.

9. See T. Wilson Dickinson, *The Green Good News: Christ's Path to Sustainable and Joyful Life* (Eugene, OR: Cascade Books, 2019) for an extensive treatment of Jesus as an organizer of alternative communities and food economies, as a healer of bodies and relationships, and as a prophet who sought to overturn an empire and restore a more just and joyful way of life.

10. Leah D. Schade, *Creation-Crisis Preaching: Ecology, Theology, and the Pulpit* (St. Louis: Chalice Press, 2015).

11. "Season of Creation" is a four-week season of the church year that begins September 1, the Day of Prayer for Creation, and runs through October 4, the Feast of St. Francis, who is the patron saint of ecology in many traditions. The three-year lectionary focuses on different themes of Creation and the website offers suggestions for hymns, prayers, sermon ideas, and education. See https://seasonofcreation.org/.

18. Embodiment in Worship

1. Kimberly Bracken Long, *The Worshiping Body: The Art of Leading Worship* (Louisville: Westminster John Knox, 2006), 14.

2. Long, *The Worshiping Body*, 17.

3. Long, *The Worshiping Body*, 17.

19. Enclave Worship and Christ's Call for Unity

1. For more information, see the website for "Ujima Village Christian Church," https://ujimachurch.org/.

2. For more on Africana worship, see *The Africana Worship Book (Year A)*, edited by Valerie Bridgeman Davis and Safiyah Fosua (Nashville: Discipleship Resources, 2006). See also *Year B* (2007), *Year C* (2008), and *Companion to the Africana Worship Book* (2008), also edited by Bridgeman and Davis. For a detailed study on the contribution of the Black Coptic Church to Black Theology, see Leonard McKinnis, "I Am Black and Beautiful: An Examination of the Black Coptic Church as the Manifestation of Liberation Theology" (PhD diss., Loyola University Chicago, 2010). For more on Afro-Catholicism, see *Afro-Catholic Festivals in the Americas: Performance, Representation, and the Making of Black Atlantic Tradition*, ed. Cécile Fromont (University Park, PA: Penn State University Press, 2019). For a sample of Black liturgical diversity, see the websites for St. Alphonsus "Rock" Liguori Catholic Church, https://www.stalphonsusrock.org/, accessed June 25, 2020; and Union Church, http://unionboston.org/, accessed June 25, 2020.

20. Worship and Disability

1. For a fuller exploration of this argument, see Rebecca F. Spurrier, *The Disabled Church: Human Difference and the Art of Communal Worship* (New York: Fordham University Press, 2019).

2. See Lennard J. Davis, "Introduction: Disability, Normality, and Power," in *The Disability Studies Reader*, 5th ed. (New York: Routledge, 2016), 1–17.

3. Alison Kafer, *Feminist, Queer, Crip* (Bloomington: Indiana University Press, 2013), 1–24. Kafer's chapter also includes a discussion on disability studies and the medical model of disability.

4. Nancy L. Eiesland, *The Disabled God: Toward a Liberatory Theology of Disability* (Nashville: Abingdon, 1994), 70–72.

5. Eiesland, *The Disabled God*, 72–73.

6. Eiesland, *The Disabled God*, 67.

7. Eiesland, *The Disabled God*, 73–75, 90–94.

8. Don E. Saliers, *Worship as Theology: Foretaste of Glory Divine* (Nashville: Abingdon, 1994), 26–30, 199.

9. See Rosemarie Garland-Thomson, "Introduction: Living Well in a World Not Made for Us," in *About Us: Essays from the Disability Series of* The New York Times, ed. Peter Catapano and Rosemarie Garland-Thomson (New York: Liveright, 2019), xxiii.

21. Worship, Gender, and Sexuality

1. Teresa Berger, "Christian Worship and Gender Practices," in *Oxford Research Encyclopedia of Religion*, ed. John Barton (Oxford: Oxford University Press, 2015), 1, doi: https://oxfordre.com/religion/view/10.1093/acrefore/9780199340378.001.0001/acrefore-9780199340378-e-6.

2. Berger, "Christian Worship and Gender Practices," 1.

3. The definitions of the words *gender* and *sexuality* have changed greatly over time and continue to have different meanings in different contexts. Here gender includes both gender identity (how one self-identifies as female, male, both, or neither) and gender expression (how one physically presents oneself as female, male, both, or neither). Sexuality refers to sexual feelings, desires (or lack thereof), and to whom one is or is not attracted (emotionally and physically). Gender and sexuality are fluid and can change over the course of one's life. As Berger writes, "The body

is appreciated as always particular. There are only bodies at worship, and these are always gendered, but also in flux, porous, changing, and transitory" (Teresa Berger, "Gender Matters in Worship: An Ecumenical Theme across a Divided Church," *Liturgy* 30, no. 4 (2015): 42, doi: https://doi.org/10.1080/0458063X.2015.1051893).

4. Berger, "Gender Matters in Worship," 39.

5. Marjorie Procter-Smith, *In Her Own Rite: Constructing Feminist Liturgical Tradition* (n.p.: Order of Saint Luke, 2013), 50.

6. Lisa Isherwood and Elizabeth Stuart, *Introducing Body Theology* (Sheffield: Sheffield Academic Press, 1998), 52.

7. Isherwood and Stuart, *Introducing Body Theology*, 31.

8. For a helpful overview of this history, see Isherwood and Stuart, *Introducing Body Theology*, 52–77.

9. Berger, "Christian Worship and Gender Practices," 6–8.

10. Adrian Thatcher, *Redeeming Gender* (Oxford: Oxford University Press, 2016).

11. Thatcher, *Redeeming Gender*, 1.

12. Thatcher, *Redeeming Gender*, 4. It is important to note that Laqueur's theory has received criticism, with some arguing that these two theories have existed alongside each other since antiquity. See, for example, Helen King, *The One-Sex Body on Trial: The Classical and Early Modern Evidence: The History of Medicine in Context* (Farnham, VT: Ashgate, 2013).

13. Berger, "Christian Worship and Gender Practices," 3–6. See also Teresa Berger, *Gender Differences and the Making of Liturgical History: Lifting a Veil on Liturgy's Past* (Farnham, VT: Ashgate, 2011).

14. Berger, "Gender Matters in Worship," 36.

15. Berger, "Gender Matters in Worship," 36; and Berger, "Christian Worship and Gender Practices," 12–13. For reflections on the impact of gender and sexuality in preaching, see Lisa L. Thompson, *Ingenuity: Preaching as an Outsider* (Nashville: Abingdon, 2018); and Angela M. Yarber, *The Gendered Pulpit: Sex, Body, and Desire in Preaching and Worship* (Cleveland, TN: Parson's Porch Books, 2013).

16. Yasmine Haflz, "Rev. Cameron Partridge Will Be First Openly Transgender Priest to Preach at Washington National Cathedral," *Huffpost* (June 6, 2014), accessed October 1, 2020, https://www.huffpost.com/entry/transgender -priest-national-cathedral-pride_n_5459762.

17. Peter Rowe, "Transgender, Nonbinary Pastor Says, 'Let's Make the Tent as Big and as Open as We Can,'" *Los Angeles Times* (February 17, 2020), accessed October 1, 2020, https://www.latimes.com/california /story/2020-02-17/first-transgender-nonbinary-priest-ordained.

18. For an example of liturgical materials and theological reflections on same-sex marriage, see The Standing Commission on Liturgy and Music, Liturgical Resources 1: "I Will Bless You, and You Will Be a Blessing," revised and expanded edition (2015), available at https://episcopalchurch.org/files/lm_i_will_bless_you_and_you_will _be_a_blessing-marriage_liturgy.pdf. For an example of a Service of Renaming, see the Episcopal Church, "A Service of Renaming," in *The Book of Occasional Services 2018*, 120–24, available at https://www.episcopalchurch.org/files /lm_book_of_occasional_services_2018.pdf.

19. Jaci Maraschin, "Worship and the Excluded," in *Liberation Theology and Sexuality*, ed. Marcella Althaus-Reid (Aldershot, VT: Ashgate, 2006), 174–75.

20. Thatcher, *Redeeming Gender*, 4. See also Adrian Thatcher, "Gender," in *Contemporary Approaches to Sexuality*, ed. Lisa Isherwood and Dirk von der Horst (London and New York: Routledge, 2018), 29.

21. For studies on how the language we use for God affects how we think about ourselves, see Jann Aldredge-Clanton, *In Whose Image? God and Gender* (London: SCM Press, 1991); and Mark J. Cartledge, "God, Gender and Social Roles: A Study in Relation to Empirical-Theological Models of the Trinity," *Journal of Empirical Theology* 22 (2009): 117–41.

22. Stephanie A. Budwey, "'God Is the Creator of All Life and the Energy of the World': German Intersex Christians' Reflections on the Image of God and Being Created in God's Image," *Theology and Sexuality* 24, no. 2 (2018): 88, doi: https://doi.org/10.1080/13558358.2018.1463643.

23. B. K. Hipsher, "God Is a Many Gendered Thing: An Apophatic Journey to Pastoral Diversity," in *Trans/formations*, ed. Marcella Althaus-Reid and Lisa Isherwood (London: SCM Press, 2009), 100.

24. Sallie McFague, *Metaphorical Theology: Models of God in Religious Language* (Philadelphia: Fortress, 1982), 20.

25. Nicola Slee, "God-language in Public and Private Prayer: A Place for Integrating Gender, Sexuality and Faith," *Theology & Sexuality* 20, no. 3 (2014): 226, doi: https://doi.org/10.1179/1355835815Z.00000000052.

26. For an example of how one intersex person felt excluded by binary language for humans, see Stephanie A. Budwey, "What We Think Is New Is in Fact Very Old!" in *In Spirit and Truth: A Vision of Episcopal Worship*, ed. Stephanie A. Budwey, Kevin Moroney, Sylvia Sweeny, and Samuel Torvend (New York: Church Publishing, Inc., 2020). See also Siobhan Garrigan, "Queer Worship," *Theology & Sexuality* 15, no. 2 (2009): 211–30.

27. Task Force on Liturgical and Prayer Book Revision, "Expansive and Inclusive Language Guidelines," 1, https://www.episcopalcommonprayer.org/uploads/1/2/9/8/129843103/expansive-inclusive_language_guidelines_-_tflpbr_draft_11-26-19.pdf, accessed June 4, 2020.

28. Task Force on Liturgical and Prayer Book Revision, "Expansive and Inclusive Language Guidelines, 1."

29. For further discussion, see Stephanie A. Budwey, "'Draw a Wider Circle—or, Perhaps, Erase': Queer(ing) Hymnody," *The Hymn* 67, no. 2 (Spring 2016): 21–26; and Stephanie A. Budwey, "Letting the Entire Body of Christ Speak: Moving Beyond the Female/Male Binary in Liturgy," in "Der Kunst ausgesetzt," Beiträge des 5. Internationalen Kongresses für Kirchenmusik, 21.–25. Oktober 2015 in Bern, ed. Thomas Garmann and Andreas Marti (Bern: Peter Lang Verlag, 2017), 189–99.

30. This collection is available for free online at https://thehymnsociety.org/resources/songs-for-the-holy-other/.

31. For an overview of writings on the relationships between music, gender, sexuality, and theology, see Dirk von der Horst, "Music," in *Contemporary Approaches to Sexuality*, ed. Lisa Isherwood and Dirk von der Horst (London and New York: Routledge, 2018), 113–23.

32. Alisha Lola Jones, "Singing High: Black Countertenors and Gendered Sound in Gospel Performance," in *The Oxford Handbook of Voice Studies*, ed. Nina Sun Eidsheim and Katherine Meizel (Oxford: Oxford University Press, 2019), doi: https://www.oxfordhandbooks.com/view/10.1093/oxfordhb/9780199982295.001.0001/oxfordhb-9780199982295-e-20. See also Alisha Lola Jones, "Are All the Choir Directors Gay? Black Men's Sexuality and Identity in Gospel Performance," in *Issues in African American Music: Power, Gender, Race, Representation*, ed. Portia K. Maultsby and Mellonee V. Burnim (New York and London: Routledge, 2017), 216–36; and Alisha Lola Jones, *Flaming?: The Peculiar Theopolitics of Fire and Desire in Black Male Gospel Performance* (Oxford: Oxford University Press, 2020).

33. Sarah Coakley, *God, Sexuality, and the Self: An Essay "On the Trinity"* (Cambridge: Cambridge University Press, 2013), 248.

34. See Marcella Althaus-Reid, *Indecent Theology: Theological Perversions in Sex, Gender and Politics* (London: Routledge, 2000), 111; and Nicola Slee, *Seeking the Risen Christa* (London: SPCK, 2011).

35. Kittredge Cherry, "Queer Kwanzaa: Queer Black Jesus Icon Presented for African American Holiday," QSpirit, December 26, 2016, accessed June 4, 2020, http://qspirit.net/queer-kwanzaa-queer-black-jesus/. For more examples of queer religious art, see Kittredge Cherry, *Art That Dares: Gay Jesus, Woman Christ, and More* (Berkeley, CA: AndroGyne Press, 2007).

22. Latinx Wisdom for Wholistic Worship

1. Justo González, ed., *¡Alabadle! Hispanic Christian Worship* (Nashville: Abingdon, 1996), 20.

2. González, *¡Alabadle!* 22–23.

3. Pedrito U. Maynard-Reid, *Diverse Worship: African American, Caribbean, and Hispanic Perspectives* (Downers Grove, IL: InterVarsity Press, 2000), Kindle edition.

4. While Samuel Soliván lists *testimonios* and *coritos* as some of the components of Hispanic Pentecostal worship, the authors of *Latina Evangélicas* consider them part and parcel of Protestant Latin@ spirituality. See Samuel Soliván, "Hispanic Pentecostal Worship," in *¡Alabadle!*; and Loida I. Martell-Otero, Zaida Maldonado-Pérez, and

Elizabeth Conde-Frazier, *Latina Evangélicas: A Theological Survey from the Margins* (Eugene, OR: Cascade Books, 2013), 40, 132, 139. In my experience, growing up in Puerto Rico and as part of the Presbyterian Church (USA), *testimonios* and *coritos* are very common in our worship, even if it follows the general pattern of Anglo churches of the same denominations González points out in *¡Alabadle!* 13.

5. Maynard-Reid, *Diverse Worship*, Kindle location 1877.

6. Martell-Otero et al., *Latina Evangélicas*, 139.

7. Maldonado-Pérez, *Latina Evangélicas*, 61.

8. In Maynard-Reid's assessment, "The theology is usually shallow, but there are exceptions." See Maynard-Reid, *Diverse Worship*, Kindle location 2543. The critique must not be taken lightly, however. Deep analysis of a song's lyrics is essential for sound theological expression, whether in writing, oratory, or songs.

9. Jonathan García-Rodríguez, "Introduction to Worship Course" class discussion, McCormick Theological Seminary, Chicago, IL, October 22, 2019.

10. Carmelo Álvarez, *El ministerio de la adoración cristiana: Teología y práctica desde la óptica protestante* (Nashville: Abingdon, 2012), 58–69.

11. Martell-Otero et al., *Latina Evangélicas*, 40.

12. Maynard-Reid, *Diverse Worship*, Kindle location 1946.

13. Maynard-Reid, *Diverse Worship*, Kindle locations 1941–1958. See also, González, *¡Alabadle!* 23.

14. González, *¡Alabadle!* 23.

15. See, among others, Lis Valle-Ruiz, "Toward Postcolonial Liturgical Preaching: Drawing on the Pre-Columbian Caribbean Religion of the Taínos," *Homiletic (Online)* 40, no. 1 (2015): 28–37; Diana Taylor, "Scenes of Cognition: Performance and Conquest," *Theatre Journal* 56, no. 3 (2004): 353–72; and Diana Taylor, *The Archive and the Repertoire: Performing Cultural Memory in the Americas* (Durham, NC: Duke University Press, 2003), chapter 1.

16. Maynard-Reid, *Diverse Worship*, Kindle locations 1989–1991, 2014–2015.

23. Worship and Whiteness

1. Brian Bantum, *Redeeming Mulatto* (Waco: Baylor University Press, 2010), 142.

2. Rebecca Anne Goetz, *The Baptism of Early Virginia: How Christianity Created Race* (Baltimore: Johns Hopkins University Press, 2012).

3. Cláudio Carvalhaes, *Liturgy in Postcolonial Perspectives: Only One Is Holy* (New York: Palgrave Macmillan, 2015), 4.

4. For further reading about the role of worship in contesting racial hierarchies and contributing to the survival of racialized minorities, see James Cone, "Sanctification, Liberation, and Black Worship," *Theology Today* 35, no. 2 (July 1, 1978): 139–52; George Garrelts, "Black Power and Black Liturgy," *Journal of Religious Thought* 39 (Spring–Summer 1983): 34–45; Scott Haldeman, *Toward Liturgies that Reconcile: Race and Ritual among African-American and European-American Protestants* (New York: Routledge, 2007).

5. For further reading about color-blind racism, see Eduardo Bonilla-Silva, *Racism without Racists: Color-Blind Racism and the Persistence of Racial Inequality in America* (New York: Rowman & Littlefield, 2017). See also Michelle Alexander, *The New Jim Crow: Mass Incarceration in the Age of Colorblindness* (New York: The New Press, 2010). I am concerned about the ableist dimensions of the terms "color-blind" and "color blindness," and the ways in which these phrasings can appeal to conceptions that are utopic. However, I concede here because engaging the aspiration or concept of colorblindness is essential to understanding racism in recent decades in the context of the US.

24. Intercultural Worship

1. Interview with Martin Luther King Jr., *Meet the Press*, April 17, 1960. http://okra.stanford.edu/transcription/document_images/Vol05Scans/17Apr1960_InterviewonMeetthePress.pdf.

2. Agnes M. Brazal and Emmanuel S. De Guzman, *Intercultural Church: Bridge of Solidarity in the Migration Context* (n.p.: Borderless, 2015), 47–48.

25. The Call for African American Worship

1. To learn more about the different perspectives of the Black church in America see Sylvester Johnson, *African American Religions 1500–2000* (New York: Cambridge University Press, 2015); Eddie Glaude Jr., *African American Religion: A Very Short Introduction* (New York: Oxford University Press, 2014); Albert Raboteau, *Canaan Land: A Religious History of African Americans* (New York: Oxford University Press, 2001).

2. Saaidiya Hartman, *Scenes of Subjection: Terror, Slavery, and Self-Making in Nineteenth-Century America* (New York: Oxford University Press, 1997), 65.

3. Melva Wilson Costen, *African American Christian Worship* (Nashville: Abingdon, 1993, 2007).

4. Albert Raboteau, *Slave Religion and the "Invisible Institution" in the Antebellum South* (New York: Oxford University Press, 1980), 218.

5. Leah Gunning Francis, *Ferguson and Faith: Sparking Leadership and Awakening Community* (St. Louis: Chalice Press, 2015), 9–10.

6. Costen, *African American Christian Worship*, 28.

26. Asian American Considerations

1. Russell Yee, *Worship on the Way: Exploring Asian North American Christian Experience* (Valley Forge, PA: Judson Press, 2012), xii–xiii.

2. Yee, *Worship on the Way*, xii–xiii.

3. Lim Swee Hong and Lester Ruth, *Lovin' on Jesus: A Concise History of Contemporary Music* (Nashville: Abingdon, 2017), 82–85.

4. Jerry Z. Park, "Assessing the Sociological Study of Asian American Christianity," *Society of Asian North American Christian Studies Journal* 1 (2009): 58.

5. "Asian Americans: A Mosaic of Faiths," Pew Research Center: Religion and Public Life, last modified July 19, 2010, https://www.pewforum.org/2012/07/19/asian-americans-a-mosaic-of-faiths-overview/.

6. The authors thank a Vanderbilt Divinity School student from fall 2020 for helping us to make the etymological clarification regarding *tongsung kido*.

7. Ruth Duck, *Worship for the Whole People of God: Vital Worship for the 21st Century* (Louisville: Westminster John Knox, 2013), 43.

8. Duck, *Worship for the Whole People of God*, 43.

9. For a couple of examples, see the websites for Starkville Chinese Christian Church (http://sccc-ms.org/drupal/) and Faith Tamil Lutheran Church (http://faithtamiltroy.org/), last accessed May 13, 2020.

10. Eunjoo Mary Kim, *Christian Preaching and Worship in Multicultural Contexts: A Practical Theological Approach* (Collegeville, MN: Liturgical, 2017), 188.

11. Viet Thanh Nguyen, *Race and Resistance: Literature and Politics in Asian America* (New York: Oxford University Press, 2002), vi.

12. Nguyen, *Race and Resistance*, 17.

13. Paul Lim, "Historically White Christian Ministries Now Have Korean American Male Leaders," interview by Morgan Lee, podcast and transcript at *Christianity Today*, episode 203, last modified March 11, 2020, https://www.christianitytoday.com/ct/2020/march-web-only/korean-evangelicals-eugene-cho-walter-kim-julius.html.

27. Intergenerational Church Today and Tomorrow

1. Mark Chaves, *Congregations in America* (Cambridge, MA: Harvard University Press, 2004), 67.

2. Chaves, *Congregations in America*, 79.

3. Pew Research Center, "Attendance at Religious Services," https://www.pewforum.org/religious-landscape -study/attendance-at-religious-services/#demographic-information.

28. Chaplaincy: Reimagining Hospital Rituals in the Context of COVID-19

1. Wendy Cadge, *Paging God: Religion in the Halls of Medicine* (Chicago: University of Chicago Press, 2012), 140–42.

2. Cadge, *Paging God*, 182.

3. "COVID-19: Strategies to Optimize the Supply of PPE and Equipment," Centers for Disease Control and Prevention, July 16, 2020, https://www.cdc.gov/coronavirus/2019-ncov/hcp/ppe-strategy/index.html; Adrienne Dunn, "Fact Check: Are Coronavirus Patients Dying Alone in Hospitals?" *USA TODAY*, April 30, 2020, https://www.usatoday.com/story/news/factcheck/2020/04/09/fact-check-coronavirus-patients-dying-alone -hospitals/5114282002/.

4. Cadge, *Paging God*, 15.

5. Michele Shields, Allison Kestenbaum, and Laura B. Dunn, "Spiritual AIM and the Work of the Chaplain: A Model for Assessing Spiritual Needs and Outcomes in Relationship," *Palliative and Supportive Care* 13, no. 1 (2015): 79.

6. Kirsten Weir, "Grief and COVID-19: Saying Goodbye in the Age of Physical Distancing," American Psychological Association, April 6, 2020, https://www.apa.org/topics/COVID-19/grief-distance.

29. Imbuing Liturgical Awe

1. For more information on the Crescendo movement, see "Crescendo: More than Music," https://www .crescendo.org/en/network.html, accessed May 20, 2020.

2. Marcia McFee, *Think Like a Filmmaker: Sensory-Rich Worship Design for Unforgettable Messages* (Truckee, CA: Trokay Press, 2016).

30. Identifying Congregational and Community Gifts for Worship

1. This form has been adapted from Norma deWaal Malefyt and Howard Vanderwell, *Designing Worship To- gether: Models and Strategies or Worship Planning* (Herndon, VA: The Alban Institute, 2005).

31. Planning Together

1. Barbara Day Miller, *Encounters with the Holy: A Conversational Model for Worship Planning* (Herndon, VA: The Alban Institute, 2010), 11–17.

2. Sandra Maria Van Opstal, *The Next Worship: Glorifying God in a Diverse World* (Downers Grove, IL: Inter- Varsity), 74–75.

3. Van Opstal, *The Next Worship*, 74–75.

4. Van Opstal, *The Next Worship*, 92–95.

5. Norma de Waal Malefyt and Howard Vanderwell, *Designing Worship Together: Models and Strategies for Wor- ship Planning* (Herndon, VA: The Alban Institute, 2005), 5.

32. Identifying Congregational Resistance to Worship

1. Constance M. Cherry, *The Worship Architect: A Blueprint for Designing Culturally Relevant and Biblically Faithful Services* (Grand Rapids, MI: Baker Academic), 270.

2. Daniel Kahneman, *Thinking Fast and Slow* (New York: Farrar, Straus and Giroux, 2011).

33. The Arts

1. Chaves, *Congregations in America*, 181.

2. Chaves, *Congregations in America*, 168.

3. Chaves, *Congregations in America*, 168.

4. Jacob D. Myers, *Curating Church: Strategies for Innovative Worship* (Nashville: Abingdon, 2018), xv.

34. Music

1. For more about the variety of "musics," see Bruno Nettl, "Is Music the Universal Language of Mankind? Commonalities and the Origins of Music" and "A Nonuniversal Language: On the Musics of the World," in *The Study of Ethnomusicology: Thirty-Three Discussions* (Urbana: University of Illinois Press, 2015), 31–48, 63–71.

2. Kathleen Marie Higgins, *The Music Between Us* (Chicago; London: The University of Chicago Press, 2012), 97.

3. Edward Foley, *Foundations of Christian Music: The Music of Pre-Constantinian Christianity* (Collegeville, MN: Liturgical, 1996), 82.

4. Cherry, *The Worship Architect*, 179.

5. Swee Hong Lim and Lester Ruth, *Lovin' on Jesus: A Concise History of Contemporary Music* (Nashville: Abingdon, 2017), 2–3. Hong and Ruth list "nine qualities of contemporary music" that include "using contemporary, nonarchaic English, using musical styles from current types of popular music," "predilection for informality," and "a reliance upon electronic technology."

36. Relevance as a Crucial Question

1. Melva Costen, *African American Christian Worship* (Nashville: Abingdon, 2007), 109.

2. Peter C. Phan, "Liturgical Inculturation: Unity in Diversity in the Postmodern Age," in *Liturgy in a Postmodern World*, ed. Keith F. Pecklers (New York: Continuum, 2003), 55.

3. Phan, "Liturgical Inculturation," 173.

4. Phan, "Liturgical Inculturation," 173.

5. Phan, "Liturgical Inculturation," 62–63.

6. See also Homi K. Bhabha, *The Location of Culture* (London: Routledge, 1994), 227.

37. Who Are the People?

1. Barbara A. Holmes, *Joy Unspeakable: Contemplative Practices of the Black Church* (Minneapolis: Fortress, 2004), 22.

38. A Chance to Start Church Over

1. Albert J. Raboteau, *Canaan Land: A Religious History of African Americans* (New York: Oxford University Press, 2001).

2. Shannon Craigo-Snell, *The Empty Church* (New York: Oxford University Press, 2014), 116.

39. How Then Shall We Gather? Pastor Reflections on Virtual Worship

1. James F. White, *Introduction to Christian Worship*, 3rd ed. (Nashville: Abingdon, 2000), Kindle location 354.

2. John Wesley, "Sermon 16: The Means of Grace," Paragraph V.1 (Northwest Nazarene University: The Wesley Center Online), http://wesley.nnu.edu/john-wesley/the-sermons-of-john-wesley-1872-edition/sermon-16-the-means-of-grace/. See also, Paragraph II.1.

3. John Calvin, *Institutes of Christian Religion* (Philadelphia: Westminster, 1960), 1192.

Conclusion: Revelation

1. For two excellent primers on congregational prayer, see Laurence H. Stookey, *Let the Whole Church Say Amen!: A Guide for Those Who Pray in Public* (Nashville: Abingdon, 2001); and Samuel Wells and Abigail Kocher, *Shaping the Prayers of the People: The Art of Intercession* (Grand Rapids, MI: Eerdmans, 2014). Stookey's work is also a workbook and especially suited for swift application.

BIBLIOGRAPHY

Introduction: The Work of the People

Agamben, Giorgio. *The Omnibus Homo Sacer*. Palo Alto, CA: Stanford University Press, 2017.

Knausgaard, Karl Ove. *My Struggle: Book I*. New York: Farrar, Straus and Giroux, 2009.

Troeger, Thomas H., and Leonora Tubbs Tisdale. *A Sermon Workbook: Exercises in the Art and Craft of Preaching*. Nashville: Abingdon, 2013.

2. The Mystery of Our Jewish Roots

Chrysostom, John. Discourses against *Judaizing Christians*, 1.3.1. Washington, DC: Catholic University Press, 1979.

Gager, John G. *Who Made Early Christianity: The Jewish Lives of the Apostle Paul*. New York: Columbia University Press, 2015.

Nixey, Catherine. *The Darkening Age: The Christian Destruction of the Classical World*. London: Macmillan, 2017.

Osiek, Carolyn, and Margaret Y. MacDonald, with Janet H. Tulloch. *A Woman's Place: House Churches in Earliest Christianity*. Minneapolis: Fortress, 2005.

Winner, Lauren. *The Dangers of Christian Practice: On Wayward Gifts, Characteristic Damage, and Sin*. New Haven, CT: Yale University Press, 2018.

Zauzmer, Julie. "The Alleged Synagogue Shooter Was a Churchgoer Who Talked Christian Theology, Raising Tough Questions for Evangelical Pastors." *The Washington Post*, May 1, 2019. https://www.washingtonpost.com/religion/2019/05/01/alleged-synagogue-shooter -was-churchgoer-who-articulated-christian-theology-prompting-tough-questions -evangelical-pastors/.

3. Liturgical Time

Bradshaw, Paul, ed. *The New Westminster Dictionary of Liturgy and Worship*. Louisville and London: Westminster John Knox, 2002.

Connell, Martin. "Pentecost." In *The New Westminster Dictionary of Liturgy and Worship*. Edited by Paul F. Bradshaw. Louisville: Westminster John Knox, 2002.

Knapp, Robert. *The Dawn of Christianity: People and Gods in a Time of Magic and Miracles*. Cambridge, MA: Harvard University Press, 2017.

Mosshammer, Alden A. *The Easter Computus and the Origins of the Christian Era*. New York: Oxford University Press, 2008.

4. Tradition

Bradshaw, Paul. *Early Christian Worship: A Basic Introduction to Ideas and Practice*. Collegeville, MN: Liturgical Press, 2010.

Bradshaw, Paul, Maxwell Johnson, and Edward L. Phillips. *The Apostolic Tradition*. Minneapolis: Fortress, 2002.

Johnson, Maxwell E. "The Apostolic Tradition." In *The Oxford History of Christian Worship*. Edited by Geoffrey Wainwright and Karen B. Westerfield Tucker, 32–75. New York: Oxford University Press, 2006.

Johnson, Maxwell E. "Imagining Early Christian Liturgy: The Traditio Apostolica—a Case Study." In *Liturgy's Imagined Past/s: Methodologies and Materials in the Writing of Liturgical History Today*. Edited by Teresa Berger and Bryan D. Spinks. Collegeville, MN: Liturgical Press, 2016.

Taft, Robert. *Beyond East and West: Problems in Liturgical Understanding*. Washington, DC: Pastoral Press, 1984.

Westerfield Tucker, Karen B. *American Methodist Worship*. Oxford: Oxford University Press, 2001.

5. The Inscrutable Preference for Two Patterns

Alikin, Valeriy A. *The Earliest History of the Christian Gathering: Origin, Development, and Content of the Christian Gathering in the First to Third Centuries*. Leiden: Brill, 2010.

de Jonge, H. J. "The Early History of the Lord's Supper," in *Religious Identity and the Invention of Tradition*, eds. J. W. van Henten and A. Houtepen. Assen: Van Gorcum, 2001, 209–37.

Fitzgerald, Francis. *The Evangelicals: The Struggle to Shape America*. New York: Simon & Schuster, 2017.

Klinghardt, M. Gemeinschaftsmahl und Mahlgemeinschaft. *Soziologie und Liturgie frühchristlicher Mahlfeiern*. Tübingen/Basel: Francke, 1996.

Lathrop, Gordon. *Holy Things: A Liturgical Theology*. Minneapolis: Fortress, 1998.

Lim, Swee Hong, and Lester Ruth. *Lovin' On Jesus: A Concise History of Contemporary Worship*. Nashville: Abingdon, 2017.

Marti, Gerardo. *Worship across the Racial Divide: Religious Music and the Multiracial Congregation*. New York: Oxford University Press, 2012.

Moore-Keish, Martha. "The Importance of Worship that Centers on the Ordo." *Liturgy* 21, no. 2 (May 2006): 15–23.

Ruth, Lester, ed. *Flow: The Ancient Way to Do Contemporary Worship*. Nashville: Abingdon, 2020.

Smith, Dennis. *From Symposium to Eucharist: The Banquet in the Early Christian World*. Minneapolis: Fortress, 2003.

Williams, Rowan. "Naming the World: Liturgy and the Transformation of Time and Matter." In *Full of Your Glory: Liturgy, Cosmos, Creation*. Edited by Teresa Berger, 23–37. Collegeville, MN: Liturgical Press, 2018.

7. Other Sacred Texts

"The African American Lectionary: A Collaborative Project of The African American Pulpit and American Baptist College of Nashville," in http://www.theafricanamericanlectionary.org /about.asp.

8. Interreligious Dialogue

Black, Kathleen (Kathy), with Bishop Kyrillos, Jonathan L. Friedmann, and Tamar Frankiel, Hamid Mavani and Jihad Turk. *Rhythms of Religious Ritual: The Yearly Cycles of Jews, Christians, and Muslims*. Claremont, CA: Claremont Press, 2018.

Schoenberg, Shira. "Ashkenazism." In Jewish Virtual Library. https://www.jewishvirtuallibrary.org/ashkenazim.

"Sunnis and Shia: Islam's Ancient Schism." BBC News, January 4, 2016, https://www.bbc.com/news/world-middle-east-16047709.

Weiner, Rebecca. "Sephardim." In Jewish Virtual Library. https://www.jewishvirtuallibrary.org/sephardim.

9. The Sacraments—Baptism

Williams, Rowan. *Being Christian: Baptism, Bible, Eucharist, and Prayer*. Grand Rapids, MI: Eerdmans, 2014.

10. The Sacraments—Eucharist

Berger, Teresa. @Worship: Liturgical Practices in Digital Worlds. New York: Routledge, 2018.

Bradshaw, Paul F. *Reconstructing Early Christian Worship*. Collegeville, MN: Pueblo, 2009.

Daily, Ruth Ann. "Church Should Weather Harsh Words." *Pittsburgh Post-Gazette*, May 29, 2002.

Liu, Gerald C. "Christmas Eve Communion: A Story of Sacramental Recovery." *Worship Arts*, November–December 2015, 7–9.

11. Preaching

Smith, Ted. "How to Preach without Notes." https://www.sermoncentral.com/pastors-preaching-articles/ted-smith-how-to-preach-without-notes-1531.

Stewart-Sykes, Alistair. *From Prophecy to Preaching: A Search for the Origins of Christian Homily*. Leiden: Brill, 2001.

Troeger, Thomas H. *The End of Preaching*. Nashville: Abingdon, 2018.

12. Languages of Liturgy and Worship

Chauvet, Louis-Marie. "Are the Words of the Liturgy Worn Out? What Diagnosis? What Pastoral Approach?" Paper presented at the North American Academy of Liturgy Annual Meeting, Baltimore, MD, January 4, 2009.

Wainwright, Geoffrey. *Doxology: The Praise of God in Worship, Doctrine, and Life*. New York: Oxford University Press, 1980.

Walton, Janet R. *Feminist Liturgy: A Matter of Justice*. Collegeville, MN: Liturgical Press, 2000.

13. Weddings

"The Knot 2019 Real Weddings Study." The Knot. https://www.wedinsights.com/report/the-knot-real-weddings.

Jennings, Willie James. *Acts: A Theological Commentary on the Bible*. Louisville: Westminster John Knox Press, 2017.

Reynolds, Philip L. *How Christian Marriage Became One of the Sacraments: The Sacramental Theology of Marriage from Its Medieval Origins to the Council of Trent*. Cambridge: Cambridge University Press, 2016.

14. Funerals

Long, Thomas G. *Accompany Them with Singing: The Christian Funeral.* Louisville: Westminster John Knox Press, 1994.

15. Other Occasional Services

Reynolds, Susan Bigelow. "From the Site of the Empty Tomb: Approaching the Hidden Grief of Prenatal Loss." *New Theology Review* 28, no. 2 (March 2016): 47–59.

United States Conference of Catholic Bishops. "Blessing of Parents after a Miscarriage or Stillbirth," https://www.usccb.org/prayer-and-worship/sacraments-and-sacramentals/bereavement-and-funerals/blessing-of-parents-after-a-miscarriage-or-stillbirth, last accessed May 27, 2020.

16. Sacred Space

Elkins, Heather Murray. Review of *Worship Space Acoustics: 3 Decades of Design.* Edited by David T. Bradley, Erica E. Ryherd, and Lauren M. Ronsse. *Homiletic* 42:1.

Kilde, Jeanne Halgren. *Sacred Power, Sacred Space: An Introduction to Christian Architecture and Worship.* New York: Oxford University Press, 2008.

Smith, Jonathan Z. *To Take Place: Toward Theory in Ritual.* Chicago and London: University of Chicago Press, 1987.

White, James F., and Susan J. White. *Church Architecture: Building and Renovating for Christian Worship.* Akron, OH: OSL Publications, 1998, 2002.

Thurman, Howard. *The Inward Journey.* Richmond, IN: Friends United Press, 1961.

17. Ecology and Worship

California Department of Forestry and Fire Protection. "2017 Wildfire Activity Statistics." April 2019, 1. https://www.fire.ca.gov/media/10059/2017_redbook_final.pdf.

Dickinson, T. Wilson. *The Green Good News: Christ's Path to Sustainable and Joyful Life.* Eugene, OR: Cascade Books, 2019.

Duck, Ruth. *Worship for the Whole People of God: Vital Worship for the 21st Century.* Louisville: Westminster John Knox, 2013.

Jabr, Ferris. "How Humanity Unleashed a Flood of New Diseases." *New York Times,* June 17, 2020. https://www.nytimes.com/2020/06/17/magazine/animal-disease-COVID.html?action=click&auth=login-email&login=email&module=Editors%20Picks&pgtype=Homepage.

Jones, Robert P., Daniel Cox, and Juhem Navarro-Rivera. *Believers, Sympathizers, and Skeptics: Why Americans Are Conflicted about Climate Change, Environmental Policy, and Science: Findings from the PRRI/AAR Religion, Values, and Climate Change Survey.* Washington, DC: Public Religion Research Institute and American Academy of Religion, 2014.

Schade, Leah D. *Creation-Crisis Preaching: Ecology, Theology, and the Pulpit.* St. Louis: Chalice Press, 2015.

Schade, Leah D. *For the Beauty of the Earth: A Lenten Devotional.* St. Louis: Chalice Press, 2019.

Sleeth, Matthew. *Reforesting Faith: What Trees Teach Us about the Nature of God and His Love for Us.* New York: Waterbrook, 2019.

Stewart, Benjamin. *A Watered Garden: Christian Worship and Earth's Ecology.* Minneapolis: Augsburg Fortress, 2011.

18. Embodiment in Worship

Long, Kimberly Bracken. *The Worshiping Body: The Art of Leading Worship*. Louisville: Westminster John Knox Press, 2006.

19. Enclave Worship and Christ's Call for Unity

Davis, Valerie Bridgeman, and Safiyah Fosua, eds. *The Africana Worship Book (Year A)*. Nashville: Discipleship Resources, 2006.

Davis, Valerie Bridgeman, and Safiyah Fosua, eds. *The Africana Worship Book (Year B)*. Nashville: Discipleship Resources, 2007.

Davis, Valerie Bridgeman, and Safiyah Fosua, eds. *The Africana Worship Book (Year C)*. Nashville: Discipleship Resources, 2008.

Davis, Valerie Bridgeman, and Safiyah Fosua, eds. *Companion to the Africana Worship Book*. Nashville: Discipleship Resources, 2008.

Fromont, Cécile, ed. *Afro-Catholic Festivals in the Americas: Performance, Representation, and the Making of Black Atlantic Tradition*. University Park: Penn State University Press, 2019.

McKinnis, Leonard. "I Am Black and Beautiful: An Examination of the Black Coptic Church as the Manifestation of Liberation Theology." PhD diss., Loyola University Chicago, 2010.

20. Worship and Disability

Catapano, Peter, and Rosemarie Garland-Thomson, eds. *About Us: Essays from the Disability Series of the* New York Times. New York: Liveright, 2019.

Davis, Lennard J. "Introduction: Disability, Normality, and Power." In *The Disability Studies Reader*, 5th ed. New York: Routledge, 2016.

Eiesland, Nancy L. *The Disabled God: Toward a Liberatory Theology of Disability*. Nashville: Abingdon, 1994.

Kafer, Alison. *Feminist, Queer, Crip*. Bloomington: Indiana University Press, 2013.

Saliers, Don E. *Worship as Theology: A Foretaste of Glory Divine*. Nashville: Abingdon, 1994.

Spurrier, Rebecca F. *The Disabled Church: Human Difference and the Art of Communal Worship*. New York: Fordham University Press, 2019.

21. Worship, Gender, and Sexuality

Aldredge-Clanton, Jann. *In Whose Image? God and Gender*. London: SCM Press, 1991.

Althaus-Reid, Marcella. *Indecent Theology: Theological Perversions in Sex, Gender and Politics*. London: Routledge, 2000.

Berger, Teresa. "Christian Worship and Gender Practices." In *Oxford Research Encyclopedia of Religion*. Edited by John Barton. Oxford: Oxford University Press, 2015, 1. doi: https://oxfordre.com/religion/view/10.1093/acrefore/9780199340378.001.0001/acrefore-9780199340378-e-6.

Berger, Teresa. *Gender Differences and the Making of Liturgical History: Lifting a Veil on Liturgy's Past*. Farnham, VT: Ashgate, 2011.

Berger, Teresa. "Gender Matters in Worship: An Ecumenical Theme across a Divided Church." *Liturgy* 30, no. 4 (2015): 42. doi: https://doi.org/10.1080/0458063X.2015.1051893.

Budwey, Stephanie A. "'Draw a Wider Circle—or, Perhaps, Erase': Queer(ing) Hymnody." *The Hymn* 67, no. 2 (Spring 2016): 21–26.

Budwey, Stephanie A. "'God Is the Creator of All Life and the Energy of the World': German Intersex Christians' Reflections on the Image of God and Being Created in God's Image." *Theology & Sexuality* 24, no. 2 (2018): 88, doi: https://doi.org/10.1080/13558358.2018.1463643.

Budwey, Stephanie A. "Letting the Entire Body of Christ Speak: Moving beyond the Female/Male Binary in Liturgy." In "Der Kunst ausgesetzt." Beiträge des 5. Internationalen Kongresses für Kirchenmusik, 21–25. Oktober 2015 in Bern, edited by Thomas Garmann and Andreas Marti, 189–99. Bern: Peter Lang Verlag, 2017.

Budwey, Stephanie A. "What We Think Is New Is in Fact Very Old!" In *In Spirit and Truth: A Vision of Episcopal Worship*, edited by Stephanie A. Budwey, Kevin Moroney, Sylvia Sweeny, and Samuel Torvend. New York: Church Publishing, Inc., 2020.

Cartledge, Mark J. "God, Gender and Social Roles: A Study in Relation to Empirical-Theological Models of the Trinity." *Journal of Empirical Theology* 22 (2009): 117–41.

Cherry, Kittredge. *Art that Dares: Gay Jesus, Woman Christ, and More.* Berkeley, CA: AndroGyne Press, 2007.

Cherry, Kittredge. "Queer Kwanzaa: Queer Black Jesus Icon Presented for African American Holiday." QSpirit. December 26, 2016. http://qspirit.net/queer-kwanzaa-queer-black-jesus/, accessed June 4, 2020.

Coakley, Sarah. *God, Sexuality, and the Self: An Essay "On the Trinity."* Cambridge: Cambridge University Press, 2013.

The Episcopal Church. "A Service of Renaming." In *The Book of Occasional Services 2018*, 120–24, https://www.episcopalchurch.org/files/lm_book_of_occasional_services_2018.pdf.

Garrigan, Siobhán. "Queer Worship." *Theology & Sexuality* 15, no. 2 (2009): 211–30.

Hipsher, B. K. "God Is a Many Gendered Thing: An Apophatic Journey to Pastoral Diversity." In *Trans/formations*. Edited by Marcella Althaus-Reid and Lisa Isherwood. London: SCM Press, 2009.

Isherwood, Lisa, and Elizabeth Stuart. *Introducing Body Theology.* Sheffield: Sheffield Academic Press, 1998.

Jones, Alisha Lola. "Are All the Choir Directors Gay? Black Men's Sexuality and Identity in Gospel Performance." In *Issues in African American Music: Power, Gender, Race, Representation*, edited by Portia K. Maultsby and Mellonee V. Burnim, 216–36. New York and London: Routledge, 2017.

Jones, Alisha Lola. *Flaming?: The Peculiar Theopolitics of Fire and Desire in Black Male Gospel Performance.* Oxford: Oxford University Press, 2020.

Jones, Alisha Lola. "Singing High: Black Countertenors and Gendered Sound in Gospel Performance." In *The Oxford Handbook of Voice Studies*, edited by Nina Sun Eidsheim and Katherine Meizel. Oxford: Oxford University Press, 2019. doi: https://www.oxfordhandbooks.com/view/10.1093/oxfordhb/9780199982295.001.0001/oxfordhb-9780199982295-e-20.

King, Helen. *The One-Sex Body on Trial: The Classical and Early Modern Evidence (The History of Medicine in Context).* Farnham, VT: Ashgate, 2013.

Maraschin, Jaci. "Worship and the Excluded." In *Liberation Theology and Sexuality*, edited by Marcella Althaus-Reid. Aldershot, VT: Ashgate, 2006.

McFague, Sallie. *Metaphorical Theology: Models of God in Religious Language.* Philadelphia: Fortress, 1982.

Procter-Smith, Marjorie. *In Her Own Rite: Constructing Feminist Liturgical Tradition.* Order of Saint Luke, 2013.

Slee, Nicola. "God-language in Public and Private Prayer: A Place for Integrating Gender, Sexuality and Faith." *Theology & Sexuality* 20, no. 3 (2014): 226. doi: https://doi.org/10.1179/135 5835815Z.00000000052.

Slee, Nicola. *Seeking the Risen Christa*. London: SPCK, 2011.

The Standing Commission on Liturgy and Music, Liturgical Resources 1: "I Will Bless You, and You Will Be a Blessing," rev. and exp. ed., 2015. https://episcopalchurch.org/files/lm_i _will_bless_you_and_you_will_be_a_blessing-marriage_liturgy.pdf.

Task Force on Liturgical and Prayer Book Revision. "Expansive & Inclusive Language Guidelines," 1. https://www.episcopalcommonprayer.org/uploads/1/2/9/8/129843103/expansive -inclusive_language_guidelines_-_tflpbr_draft_11-26-19.pdf.

Thatcher, Adrian. "Gender." In *Contemporary Approaches to Sexuality*, edited by Lisa Isherwood and Dirk von der Horst. London and New York: Routledge, 2018.

Thatcher, Adrian. *Redeeming Gender*. Oxford: Oxford University Press, 2016.

Thompson, Lisa L. *Ingenuity: Preaching as an Outsider*. Nashville: Abingdon, 2018.

von der Horst, Dirk. "Music." In *Contemporary Approaches to Sexuality*, edited by Lisa Isherwood and Dirk von der Horst, 113–23. London and New York: Routledge, 2018.

Yarber, Angela M. *The Gendered Pulpit: Sex, Body, and Desire in Preaching and Worship*. Cleveland, TN: Parson's Porch Books, 2013.

22. Latinx Wisdom for Wholistic Worship

Álvarez, Carmelo. *El ministerio de la adoración cristiana: Teología y práctica desde la óptica protestante*. Nashville: Abingdon, 2012.

González, Justo, ed. *¡Alabadle! Hispanic Christian Worship*. Nashville: Abingdon, 1996.

Martell-Otero, Loida I., Zaida Maldonado-Pérez, and Elizabeth Conde-Frazier. *Latina Evangélicas: A Theological Survey from the Margins*. Eugene, OR: Cascade Books, 2013.

Maynard-Reid, Pedrito U. *Diverse Worship: African American, Caribbean, and Hispanic Perspectives*. Downers Grove, IL: InterVarsity Press, 2000. Kindle.

Taylor, Diana. *The Archive and the Repertoire: Performing Cultural Memory in the Americas*. Durham, NC: Duke University Press, 2003.

Taylor, Diana. "Scenes of Cognition: Performance and Conquest." *Theatre Journal* 56, no. 3 (2004): 353–72.

Valle-Ruiz, Lis. "Toward Postcolonial Liturgical Preaching: Drawing on the Pre-Columbian Caribbean Religion of the Taínos." *Homiletic (Online)* 40, no. 1 (2015): 28–37.

23. Worship and Whiteness

Alexander, Michelle. *The New Jim Crow: Mass Incarceration in the Age of Colorblindness*. New York: The New Press, 2010.

Bantum, Brian. *Redeeming Mulatto*. Waco: Baylor University Press, 2010.

Bonilla-Silva, Eduardo. *Racism without Racists: Color-Blind Racism and the Persistence of Racial Inequality in America*. New York: Rowman & Littlefield, 2017.

Carvalhaes, Cláudio. *Liturgy in Postcolonial Perspectives: Only One Is Holy*. New York: Palgrave Macmillan, 2015.

Cone, James. "Sanctification, Liberation, and Black Worship." *Theology Today* 35, no. 2 (July 1, 1978): 139–52.

Garrelts, George. "Black Power and Black Liturgy." *Journal of Religious Thought* 39 (Spring–Summer 1983): 34–45.

Goetz, Rebecca Anne. *The Baptism of Early Virginia: How Christianity Created Race*. Baltimore: Johns Hopkins University Press, 2012.

Haldeman, Scott. *Toward Liturgies that Reconcile: Race and Ritual among African-American and European-American Protestants*. New York: Routledge, 2007.

24. Intercultural Worship

Brazal, Agnes M., and Emmanuel S. De Guzman. *Intercultural Church: Bridge of Solidarity in the Migration Context*. N.p.: Borderless, 2015.

Marzouk, Safwat. *Intercultural Church: A Biblical Vision in an Age of Migration*. Minneapolis: Fortress, 2019.

Meet the Press. "Interview with Martin Luther King Jr.," April 17, 1960, http://okra.stanford.edu /transcription/document_images/Vol05Scans/17Apr1960_InterviewonMeetthePress.pdf.

Van Opstal, Sandra Maria. *The Next Worship: Glorifying God in a Diverse World*. Downers Grove, IL: IVP Books, 2015.

25. The Call for African American Worship

Costen, Melva. *African American Christian Worship*. Nashville: Abingdon, 1993, 2007.

Francis, Leah Gunning. *Ferguson and Faith: Sparking Leadership and Awakening Community*. St. Louis: Chalice Press, 2015.

Glaude, Eddie, Jr. *African American Religion: A Very Short Introduction*. New York: Oxford University Press, 2014.

Hartman, Saaidiya. *Scenes of Subjection: Terror, Slavery, and Self-Making in Nineteenth-Century America*. New York: Oxford University Press, 1997.

Johnson, Sylvester. *African American Religions 1500–2000*. New York: Cambridge University Press, 2015.

Raboteau, Albert. *Canaan Land: A Religious History of African Americans*. New York: Oxford University Press, 2001.

Raboteau, Albert. *Slave Religion and the "Invisible Institution" in the Antebellum South*. New York: Oxford University Press, 1980.

26. Asian American Considerations

"Asian Americans: A Mosaic of Faiths." *Pew Research Center: Religion and Public Life*. July 19, 2010. https://www.pewforum.org/2012/07/19/asian-americans-a-mosaic-of-faiths -overview/.

Kim, Eunjoo Mary. *Christian Preaching and Worship in Multicultural Contexts: A Practical Theological Approach*. Collegeville, MN: Liturgical Press, 2017.

Lim, Paul. Interview with Morgan. "Historically White Christian Ministries Now Have Korean American Male Leaders." *Christianity Today* podcast and transcript at episode 203. March 11, 2020. https://www.christianitytoday.com/ct/2020/march-web-only/korean-evangelicals -eugene-cho-walter-kim-julius.html.

Nguyen, Viet Thanh. *Race and Resistance: Literature and Politics in Asian America*. New York: Oxford University Press, 2002.

Park, Jerry Z. "Assessing the Sociological Study of Asian American Christianity." *Society of Asian North American Christian Studies Journal* 1 (2009): 57–94.

Yee, Russell. *Worship on the Way: Exploring Asian North American Christian Experience.* Valley Forge, PA: Judson Press, 2012.

27. Intergenerational Church Today and Tomorrow

Chaves, Mark. *Congregations in America.* Cambridge, MA: Harvard University Press, 2004.

Pew Research Center. "Attendance at Religious Services." https://www.pewforum.org/religious-landscape-study/attendance-at-religious-services/#demographic-information.

28. Chaplaincy: Reimagining Hospital Rituals in the Context of COVID-19

Cadge, Wendy. *Paging God: Religion in the Halls of Medicine.* Chicago: University of Chicago Press, 2012.

"COVID-19: Strategies to Optimize the Supply of PPE and Equipment." Centers for Disease Control and Prevention. May 18, 2020. https://www.cdc.gov/coronavirus/2019-ncov/hcp/ppe-strategy/index.html.

Dunn, Adrienne. "Fact Check: Are Coronavirus Patients Dying Alone in Hospitals?" *USA Today.* April 30, 2020. https://www.usatoday.com/story/news/factcheck/2020/04/09/fact-check-coronavirus-patients-dying-alone-hospitals/5114282002/.

Shields, Michele, Allison Kestenbaum, and Laura B. Dunn. "Spiritual AIM and the Work of the Chaplain: A Model for Assessing Spiritual Needs and Outcomes in Relationship." *Palliative and Supportive Care* 13, no. 1 (2015): 75–89.

Weir, Kirsten. "Grief and COVID-19: Saying Goodbye in the Age of Physical Distancing." American Psychological Association, April 6, 2020. https://www.apa.org/topics/COVID-19/grief-distance.

29. Imbuing Liturgical Awe

"Crescendo: More than Music." See https://www.crescendo.org/en/network.html, accessed May 20, 2020.

McFee, Marcia. *Think Like a Filmmaker: Sensory-Rich Worship Design for Unforgettable Messages.* Truckee, CA: Trokay Press, 2016.

30. Identifying Congregational and Community Gifts for Worship

Malefyt, Norma deWaal, and Howard Vanderwell. *Designing Worship Together: Models and Strategies or Worship Planning.* Herndon, VA: The Alban Institute, 2005.

31. Planning Together

Day Miller, Barbara. *Encounters with the Holy: A Conversational Model for Worship Planning.* Herndon, VA: The Alban Institute, 2010.

Van Opstal, Sandra Maria. *The Next Worship: Glorifying God in a Diverse World.* Downers Grove, IL: InterVarsity Press.

32. Identifying Congregational Resistance to Worship

Cherry, Constance M. *The Worship Architect: A Blueprint for Designing Culturally Relevant and Biblically Faithful Services.* Grand Rapids, MI: Baker Academic, 2010.

Kahneman, Daniel. *Thinking Fast and Slow.* New York: Farrar, Straus and Giroux, 2011.

33. The Arts

Cage, John. *Composition in Retrospect.* Cambridge, MA: Exact Change, 2008.

Foster, Susan Leigh. *Choreographing Empathy.* London: Routlege, 2011.

Kraus, Chris. *Where Art Belongs.* Los Angeles: Semiotexte, 2011.

Metropolitan Museum of Art. *The Artist Project: What Artists See When They Look at Art.* London; New York: Phaidon, 2017.

Myers, Jacob D. *Curating Church: Strategies for Innovative Worship.* Nashville: Abingdon, 2018.

Shahn, Ben. *The Shape of Content.* Cambridge, MA: Harvard University Press, 1985.

Steyerl, Hito. *Duty Free Art: Art in the Age of Planetary Civil War.* London; New York: Verso, 2017.

34. Music

Foley, Edward. *Foundations of Christian Music: The Music of Pre-Constantinian Christianity.* Collegeville, MN: Liturgical Press, 1996.

Higgins, Kathleen Marie. *The Music between Us.* Chicago; London: University of Chicago Press, 2012.

Nettl, Bruce. *The Study of Ethnomusicology: Thirty-Three Discussions.* Urbana: University of Illinois Press, 2015.

36. Relevance as a Crucial Question

Bhabha, Homi K. *The Location of Culture.* London: Routledge, 1994.

Phan, Peter C. "Liturgical Inculturation: Unity in Diversity in the Postmodern Age." In *Liturgy in a Postmodern World*, edited by Keith F. Pecklers. New York: Continuum, 2003.

37. Who Are the People?

Holmes, Barbara A. *Joy Unspeakable: Contemplative Practices of the Black Church.* Minneapolis, MN: Fortress, 2004.

38. A Chance to Start Church Over

Craigo-Snell, Shannon. *The Empty Church.* New York: Oxford University Press, 2014.

39. How Then Shall We Gather? Pastor Reflections on Virtual Worship

Calvin, John. *Institutes of Christian Religion.* Philadelphia: Westminster, 1960.

Wesley, John. "Sermon 16: The Means of Grace." Northwest Nazarene University: The Wesley Center Online. http://wesley.nnu.edu/john-wesley/the-sermons-of-john-wesley-1872-edition/sermon-16-the-means-of-grace/.

White, James F. *Introduction to Christian Worship*, 3rd ed. Nashville: Abingdon, 2000, Kindle location 354.

Conclusion: Revelation

Stookey, Laurence H. *Let the Whole Church Say Amen!: A Guide for Those Who Pray in Public.* Nashville: Abingdon, 2001.

Wells, Samuel, and Aigail Kocher. *Shaping the Prayers of the People: The Art of Intercession.* Grand Rapids, MI: Eerdmans, 2014.

Made in the USA
Middletown, DE
17 September 2021